SCHOLASTIC

D0580363

Just-Right Writing Mini-Lessons

Grades 2-3

Mini-Lessons to Teach Your Students the Essential Skills and Strategies They Need to Write Fiction and Nonfiction

by Cheryl M. Sigmon and Sylvia M. Ford

New York • Toronto • London • Auckland • Sydney
Mexico City • New Delhi • Hong Kong • Buenos Aires

Teaching *Resources*

THIS BOOK IS DEDICATED TO...

Second- and third-grade teachers who inspire their students to become writers,

Also, to Terry Cooper and Joanna Davis-Swing at Scholastic,
who saw the potential of this series to help teachers,

And, with special thanks to Merryl Maleska Wilbur, our editor, for her constantly keen eye,
guiding hands, and gentle voice in making this a better resource for all teachers,
CMS and SMF

To the memory of my loving parents, Garrett and Kathryn Mobley,
and in honor of my wonderful mother-in-law, Margaret Ford,
SMF

To my girls, Ashley, Beth, and Caroline, who have enriched my life,
and, again, to my husband Ray for his love and support of my efforts,
CMS

ACKNOWLEDGEMENTS FOR WRITING SAMPLES AND PHOTOGRAPHS:

Appoquinimink School District, Odessa, DE: Brick Mill Elementary School;
Cedar Lane Elementary School; Olive B. Loss Elementary School;
Silver Lake Elementary School; Townsend Elementary School

Greenview Elementary School, Richland District One, Columbia, SC

Harris Courson, Rosewood Elementary School, Richland District One, Columbia, SC

R. Earle Davis Elementary School, Lexington District Two, West Columbia, SC

Kokomo Center Public Schools, Kokomo, IN

Rhonda Reed, North Miami Elementary School, Denver, IN

Mentone Elementary School, Mentone, IN

Kristina Tucker and Cathy Weaver, Merriam Avenue Elementary School, Newton, NJ

Cathy Striggow, Regina Freyberger, and Patti Smith, Jefferson Elementary School, Ft. Riley, KS

Cover design by Jason Robinson.
Cover photo by David Buffington/PictureQuest.
Interior design by Solutions by Design, Inc.

ISBN: 0-439-57409-9

Table of Contents

Introduction

How to Use This Book 7

How These Mini-Lessons Were Selected 8

Sequencing Your Lessons 8

The Mini-Lessons as Part of the Writing Workshop 9

Thinking Aloud During the Mini-Lesson 10

Beyond These Lessons 11

Mini-Lessons

SECTION ONE—Teaching the Basics 14

Section Introduction 14

Drafting in acceptable format 18

Writing in complete sentences 19

Ending sentences correctly 20

Two-Part Lesson: Early Focus on Spelling

    Part 1: Preliminary planning 21

    Part 2: Spelling *no excuses words* correctly 22

Using spelling strategies for writing fluency 23

Two-Part Lesson: Using Classroom Resources for Spelling and Writing

    Part 1: Using the dictionary 24

    Part 2: Using a thesaurus 25

Using the computer to help with spelling 26

SECTION TWO—Planning for Writing 27

Section Introduction 27

Two-Part Lesson: Finding Ideas for Stories

    Part 1: Turning the ordinary into the *extra*ordinary 30

    Part 2: Ideas are where we least expect them 31

Brainstorming for ideas 32

Warming up for writing 33

Organizing with letters and numbers 34

Writing questions for investigating 35

SECTION THREE—Writing the Draft 36

Section Introduction 36

Three-Part Lesson: The Beginning, Middle, and End of It All

    Part 1: Understanding basic literary elements 39

    Parts 2 and 3: Developing the plot by adding details 40

Getting focused on a topic.. 41

Beginning with a topic sentence 42

Two-Part Lesson: Grouping Ideas Into a Paragraph

    Part 1: Planning the paragraph... 43

    Part 2: Writing the paragraph.. 44

Creating multiple paragraphs 45

Four-Part Lesson: Using Resource Materials

    Part 1: Taking notes 46

    Part 2: Taking notes 47

    Part 3: Outlining information from notes 48

    Part 4: Paraphrasing information from the outline........................ 49

Giving credit for borrowed information 50

Two-Part Lesson: Organizing Data Into Useful Formats 51

    Part 1: Organizing in visual and graphic formats 51

    Part 2: Organizing with text and visuals/graphics........................ 52

Using organizational features of printed text 53

SECTION FOUR—Making Writing Cleaner and Clearer (Conventions) 54

Section Introduction 54

Using singular and plural common and proper nouns 57

Maintaining tense 58

Using pronouns as substitutes.. 59

Using commas in a series 60

Using quotation marks.. 61

Establishing subject/verb agreement....................................... 62

Using descriptive words 63

Learning when to use apostrophes 64

Capitalizing words 65

SECTION FIVE—Making Writing Better (Revision)

Section Introduction 66

Using sequencing and time order words. 68

Using imagery in writing. 69

Three-Part Lesson: Learning From Authors

    Part 1: Using others' ideas as models 70

    Part 2: Using text structure models 71

    Part 3: Using organization models 72

Collecting interesting words 73

Working with specialized vocabulary 74

Writing to maintain consistent person 75

Varying sentence structure. 76

Creating voice in writing. 77

Using several sources 78

SECTION SIX—Writing for Real Purposes and Audiences

Section Introduction 79

Writing brief personal narratives. 82

Writing in response 83

Three-Part Lesson: Writing a Friendly Letter

    Part 1: Planning 84

    Part 2: Learning what makes a good friendly letter. 85

    Part 3: Using correct punctuation for letters and envelopes. 86

Two-Part Lesson: Writing a Persuasive Letter

    Part 1: Planning 87

    Part 2: Using the organizational plan 88

Two-Part Lesson: Writing a News Article

    Part 1: Planning 89

    Part 2: Writing the news article. 90

Writing a cinquain (unrhymed) poem 91

Learning about rhymed and unrhymed poems 92

Two-Part Lesson: Writing and Presenting a Book Report

    Part 1: Writing a summary 93

    Part 2: Interviewing a character 94

Writing in learning logs. 95

Writing directions 96

You've got mail! 97

SECTION SEVEN—Polishing and Publishing Our Writing 98

  Section Introduction 98

  Editing with resources 101

  Two Part Lesson: Using a Simple Checklist for Revising and Editing

    Part 1: Revising 102

    Part 2: Editing 103

  Using technology (word processing) 104

  Sharing writing orally with others 105

  Four-Part Lesson: Publishing a Nonfiction Book

    Part 1: Selecting a topic and getting started 106

    Parts 2 and 3: Researching and sharing 107

    Part 4: Typing and assembling 108

  Publishing in various formats 109

Appendices

  Spelling Strategies 110

  Directions for Making a Kaleidoscope 111

  Alphabet Chart 112

  Questions for investigating worksheet 113

  Writing Graphic Organizer 114

  Resource Gathering Forms 115

  Transparency Master for *The Magic School Bus* 116

  Sequencing Chart 117

  Imagery Chart 118

  Letter Puzzle #1 119

  Letter Puzzle #2 120

  Persuasive Letter Template 121

  5 Ws with Group Cut-outs (2 sets) 122

  5 Ws with Group Cut-outs (3 sets) 123

  Book-O Book Report Matrix 124

  Book Report Assessment 125

  Revision and Editing Checklist 126

Bibliography 127

Introduction

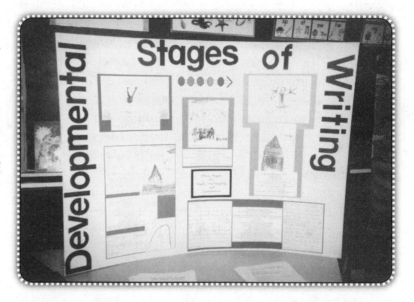

How to Use This Book

Our intent in sharing this series of mini-lesson books is to show how to integrate what needs to be taught in the area of writing at different grade levels into a powerful instructional context—real writing! Many of us were not taught how to write well when we were in school. We were given writing assignments, but our teachers rarely instructed us about the attributes of quality writing. Additionally, real writing was something that we were only permitted to do after we learned the proper mechanics, grammar, and usage to express our thoughts and ideas correctly. Our grades often reflected the level of correctness we'd achieved, regardless of the originality or development of our ideas, the richness of our figurative language, or the voice in which we wrote.

Gone are those days! Educators now realize that assigning writing doesn't teach it. Instruction needs to be direct and explicit in order to have an impact on beginning writers, and it needs to be offered in the context of something that makes sense to students—the context of real writing. Teachers also realize that correctness of conventions doesn't make writing better—only cleaner. And clean writing and good writing don't always equate.

Modeling writing daily—showing rather than telling about the attributes of effective communication—leads students to those "ah-ha!" moments of understanding: "That's why I need a comma after an introductory clause!" or "Those adjectives really help my character come alive!" or "Combining those sentences made all the difference!" We now know that daily modeling helps students transfer new knowledge to their own writing.

And so you'll find this to be a book of the daily lessons that teachers might model in short, powerful "sound-bytes" of time in the framework of a Writing Workshop. The lessons usually fit into a 10- to 15-minute time period for the modeling portion of the workshop. After you model for the class, students will have a chance to write—hopefully having absorbed some of what you have shown them. Students are *not* expected to write about what you, the teacher, write about in your modeling. They're not even expected to practice the lesson's skills that very day. These skills will be reinforced in subsequent lessons as an ongoing reminder of what constitutes good writing, and of the options available to writers.

How These Mini-Lessons Were Selected

Good instruction in the classroom is usually based on two things: 1) the needs of the students as evidenced by their writing and their conversations; and 2) the curriculum provided by the school, district, or state that defines what students should know and be able to do at that particular grade level.

As the teacher, you determine the needs of your students and use this information to shape your instruction. If most of the students demonstrate a similar need, the instruction may become a mini-lesson for the entire class. If, instead, a particular student has a unique need, you may decide to provide one-on-one instruction during an individual conference with that student. We don't pretend to know your students well enough to suggest that there is a perfect match between the mini-lessons in this book and their specific needs. However, after many years of experience, we can assure you that, with some tweaking here and there, you'll be close!

Curriculum guides also inform teachers' decisions about mini-lessons. Most teachers believe that it would be foolish not to align instruction, curriculum, and district/state assessment. Hopefully, that curriculum reflects the criteria that teachers feel represent elements of good, quality writing at their grade level.

In designing this guide, we took the curriculum guides of 11 states, representing different geographic areas around the country. We then mapped these standards to find the most common writing objectives—relevant to the second and third grades—shared among these states.

> Along with the National Standards, the standards of the following 11 states were gathered to create the curriculum for this book: California, Colorado, Missouri, Florida, Washington, South Carolina, Virginia, Indiana, Texas, Pennsylvania, and New York.

The mini-lessons in this book spring from these; they show you how to incorporate those objectives/standards into the natural context of your teaching. We attempt to show students how the use of these standards really does help their writing to be clearer and more powerful. We hope that the mini-lessons serve to motivate students to write by letting them see how easy writing is and how it can have a real effect on others.

In the first book in this mini-lesson series, aimed at first grade, children's personal experiences formed the context for most of the mini-lessons. In this book, however, the context shifts more often to connections students need to make both with literature and with the content areas they're studying—social studies, science, math, and health.

Sequencing Your Lessons

The lessons in this book do not necessarily appear in the order in which you should teach them throughout the year. Instead, they are organized by the purposes for which they are taught. With the exception of the first section—"Teaching the Basics," which should occur at the very beginning of the year—the other sections should be viewed as a menu. You may pick and choose appropriately based on your students' needs and on opportunities to integrate lessons with other content being taught.

A teacher keeps a bucket of story starters in her Publishing Center.

Consider these hints when designing the appropriate sequence of lessons in your classroom:

☆ The narrative for "Section 1: Teaching the Basics" will help you to establish basic guidelines that will support your students daily as they write. The lessons in that section show how these guidelines can be taught as mini-lessons. You'll want to start with these lessons, keeping in mind that some of your students may be ready for more sophisticated lessons, which you can intersperse with these basics.

☆ If introduced early in the year, "Section 2: Planning for Writing" and "Section 3: Writing the Draft" will demonstrate for students how they can generate their own ideas for writing and will give them some basic structure for their writing. In the beginning of the year, you'll want to be careful not to overemphasize formal planning as students begin to build fluency and confidence in their ability to write. Letting students know that writing is a basic communication skill—nothing mysterious or lofty—is one of the main goals in their early writing instruction.

☆ Mix lessons from Sections 3 through 7 throughout the year as you feel they're appropriate to support your students' growth in writing. Be sure to think about balancing lessons that deal with conventions and those that deal with revisions.

☆ We definitely do not advise teaching all of the "Making Writing Clearer and Cleaner" lessons in Section 4 in succession; doing so might convey to students that writing has to be correct to be acceptable or good. Mix lessons on grammar, mechanics, and usage with lessons from other sections.

☆ Lessons from the "Writing for Real Purposes and Audiences" section should be sprinkled throughout the year so that students develop a clear understanding that writing has real application to their everyday lives. It's not mostly an assignment of topics!

Take time to read through the Table of Contents and to think about your other content as you design the right scope and sequence of lessons for the year.

The Mini-Lessons as Part of the Writing Workshop

The Writing Workshop is traditionally divided into three parts: 1) the teacher's model lesson; 2) the students' writing time; and 3) time for students to share what they've been working on. This book deals with the first portion of time—the model lesson—although these model lessons certainly have an impact on students' writing time and on their sharing time. The first segment is a regular, daily time in which the teacher writes for students. Modeling may be done in any number of ways; typically, however, it involves the teacher sitting down to write while the students observe. Because this serves as the teacher's direct, explicit instruction, it may not be as interactive as instruction during other parts of the day.

Our favorite way to model the daily writing is to sit down beside an overhead projector, simulating as closely as possible the posture students will assume during their writing time. We face the class, allowing the students to watch and listen as we make the decisions that writers make when they compose. Think of the following list of materials and resources as standard for a large number of the mini-lessons in this book. Within each lesson, we also include a brief list of materials and resources particular to that lesson's activity. These daily materials may include:

☆ Transparencies with lines similar to the lined paper students will use.

☆ Plastic sheets in which you insert your lined transparencies.

☆ A three-ring binder to store selected writing samples that you might refer to again during the year or that you might want to save as ideas for the following year.

☆ Dividers for your binder to catalog the types of writing and the skills you teach.

☆ Transparency pens in multiple colors.

If you don't have access to an overhead projector, you can model writing on chart paper, or even on a chalkboard or dry-erase board (though this last option won't allow you to save your compositions). You'll still need pens or chalk in a variety of colors. At second and third grade, producing the model composition on a chalkboard or chart

A variety of writing tools in the Publishing Center inspire students' creativity.

becomes increasingly more cumbersome as the pieces grow in length and as they often are used over several days.

Teachers should view model lessons in second and third grade as serving several purposes, all of which are important. Your lessons will:

☆ Model how writers get their ideas.

☆ Model the basic conventions of writing.

☆ Model good writing habits.

☆ Model the writing process.

☆ Offer writing options to students.

☆ Model the application of all that students are learning at other times.

☆ Motivate students to write.

If you are a teacher who hasn't yet had experience with mini-lessons, remember the words of writing guru Nancie Atwell: "We only have to write a little better than they do for them to take away something from our demonstrations." So take a deep breath and try it. Day by day, the modeling should become easier and more enjoyable for you, and you'll quickly see how your students grow because of this experience.

Thinking Aloud During the Mini-Lesson

Just as some students don't know how to actively reflect as they read, some students don't know how to think about writing as they're composing. Modeling the decisions that a writer must make, even the little ones, will allow those same thought processes to become part of your students' habits.

As important as modeling the composition itself is modeling the mental process involved in composing. "Thinking aloud," as it's called, involves expressing aloud the decisions that writers must make as they write. For example, as you get started, you might say, "Oops! I surely can't start writing on this side of the page. I've got to turn my paper over so that I have the holes on the left side of the page to start. That's better! Okay, my name goes on the top line. I'll need to start over here on the left side to make sure my name fits in. I've got to look over at the calendar to check for today's date to write that on the next line. Now I'm ready to get started with my writing!"

If you haven't tried a "think aloud" with your students, it might seem a bit awkward at first. When aspects of writing are automatic for us as mature writers, it's sometimes difficult to slow down and think deliberately about what we're doing and why we're doing it. After practicing the think aloud for several days or several weeks, you'll soon find that it gets much easier!

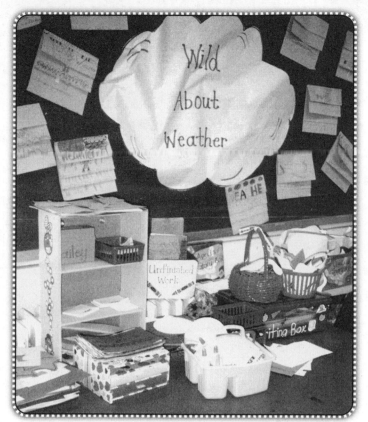

Beyond These Lessons

Writing tools and theme boards encourage young writers.

Most schools have approximately 180 days of instruction. This book offers instruction for 77 days. Even including the follow-up lesson ideas in the Quick Hints sections, a little quick math tells us that you would need to create many of your own lessons if you were to use each lesson or lesson idea once. Rarely, however, would we expect a teacher to teach the concepts and skills included in this book only once! Even with the brightest of classes, the lessons need to be retaught and reinforced often.

With that said, we also realize that you will indeed need to create lessons in addition to those in this book. Our hope is that this book will make it easier for you to design your own lessons—that it will in fact provide you with templates for those additional lessons. For example, in order to teach students how to use adjectives correctly in their writing, one direct lesson definitely does not suffice! Students need several exposures to the challenges of descriptive writing. Most of these mini-lessons offer you a sample paragraph or story to use in your initial teaching. So our recommendation is simple: just repeat the same format and create a similar composition of your own in which descriptive writing, for example, is the main focus.

Remember, too, that you'll need to consult with your own curriculum guide to be sure that you're addressing all of the standards and objectives required for your classroom. We advise that you put your curriculum guide side-by-side with our Table of Contents and/or the Matrix of Major Standards (pages 12–13) and check off the standards this book addresses. Take note of the standards that are not addressed, and fill in the gaps so that every standard or objective receives attention and direct instruction.

We sincerely hope that these mini-lessons will help make the Writing Workshop a fun time of day for you and your students.

MATRIX of MAJOR STANDARDS (See Table of Contents for Standard Subcategories)

Mini-Lesson Page Numbers

Grades 2–3 Standards

Standard	18	19	20	21–22	23	24–25	26	30–31	32	33	34	35	39–40	41	42	43–44	45	46–49	50	51–52	53	57	58
Write legibly, form letters, space words and sentences	X	X	X																				
Prewrite using graphic organizers, lists, outlines									X	X	X		X		X		X		X	X			
Focus on one topic											X			X	X	X	X		X	X			
Write using correct conventions			X	X	X	X	X															X	X
Write in complete sentences		X	X									X		X	X								
Use correct capitalization		X	X																				
Use correct spellings for freq. used words/common patterns				X	X	X	X																
Use classroom resources and strategies for spelling				X	X	X	X																
Publish variety of texts																					X		
Engage in sustained writing																X	X	X	X				
Record questions for investigating												X						X					
Write in response to what's read and written																		X		X			
Write for different purposes and audiences												X	X					X	X	X			
Use writing process: prewrite								X	X	X	X	X	X			X	X	X	X	X			
Use writing process: draft	X	X	X	X	X								X	X	X	X	X	X	X	X			
Use writing process: revise																							
Use writing process: edit						X	X															X	X
Use writing process: publish																					X		
Use technology for writing							X																

Mini-Lesson Page Numbers

59	60	61	62	63	64	65	68	69	70–72	73	74	75	76	77	78	82	83	84–86	87–88	89–90	91	92	93–94	95	96	97	101	102–103	104	105	106–108	109
																										X	X	X	X		X	X
									X		X				X	X			X	X	X	X									X	
									X							X	X	X	X	X			X	X	X						X	
X	X	X	X	X	X	X					X	X						X		X				X	X	X	X	X			X	X
		X			X								X								X			X			X	X	X		X	
					X								X				X					X		X			X	X	X		X	
																									X	X	X					
																								X	X	X	X					
																	X		X	X		X		X							X	X
																X	X	X	X		X	X	X	X							X	X
																				X			X						X			
										X			X	X	X								X	X							X	X
								X	X		X		X	X	X	X	X	X	X	X	X	X	X	X	X					X	X	
										X	X	X					X	X	X	X	X	X									X	
X								X			X		X	X	X	X			X	X			X	X	X				X		X	
X			X				X	X	X	X	X	X	X	X															X	X	X	
X	X	X			X	X																								X	X	
																					X					X					X	X
																										X	X		X		X	

Teaching the Basics

The modeling and writing that students experienced in first and, perhaps, second grade have given them a firm foundation of how phonics can help them to communicate in writing. These emergent writers have spent a great deal of time deliberating over each and every letter and sound, and have sometimes made their marks on paper with painstaking motions. The teacher's modeling has consistently conveyed that writing is a basic communication skill—that anything that can be said can also be written on paper. Students have seen daily examples of such fundamentals as:

☆ What sentences look like and how they sound.

☆ How and when uppercase letters are used.

☆ How to generate original ideas for writing.

☆ How to stay focused on a particular topic.

Students who are fortunate to have been in first-grade classrooms in which teachers allowed them daily writing time have also developed a certain amount of confidence in themselves as writers—perhaps even experiencing the exhilaration of being a "published" author through producing class and individual books.

By second and third grade—as students have grown in their ability to access and apply their language skills and have emerged into developing writers—they are ready to progress beyond the basics of phonetic application and experiments with conventions. Nonetheless, they still need to be exposed to the basic conventions daily, through good modeling provided by the teacher, so that the conventions become automatic for them as writers. As automaticity develops through daily work with the basics, students can give more of their attention to the elements that will help their writing become better, not just cleaner.

In the beginning of the year, teachers need to include the basics in their mini-lessons for two main reasons. First, it is essential to refresh students' memories, especially since they are all fairly new writers. The sophisticated process of writing calls for students to synthesize a great number of elements all at once—phonetic understanding, grammar, usage, recall of experiences, and fine motor skills in handwriting, to name a few. To continue their writing practice, students will surely need a refresher in how everything comes together on paper. Often, too, students put writing aside in the summer and need some time to get back "in the swing" of it. The constant modeling and practice at the beginning of the year will be welcomed.

Second, the teacher needs to make sure that all students have had this basic instruction in the previous grade(s). Unless students have looped with their teacher (a practice wherein students and their teacher all progress together to the next grade level), there's no guarantee that they have had the kind of instruction that will enable them to feel confident in their ability to write. Daily writing opportunities, unfortunately, are not a uniform practice in all schools or all classrooms. So while for some students the mini-lessons in basic elements are only a review, for others the lessons are actually introductory instruction.

When a teacher uses a transparency to model writing, he or she can face the class and allow students to watch and listen to the decision-making and composing processes.

All young writers in second and third grade need reassurance that no matter what their skill level, they will be accepted and encouraged as writers. The teacher's role in the beginning of the year includes validating their early attempts, motivating them to experiment in their writing, and creating a risk-taking environment—all in the instructional context of providing the basic tools necessary for good writing. This first section is intended to show you how to accomplish this.

As your year gets started, there are decisions to make before the very first mini-lesson. You need to decide what you consider to be the basics that your students should adhere to daily, even in their rough-draft writing. For example, you need to communicate clearly to students that the rough draft is just that—rough! At the same time, you need to let them know that there are both acceptable and unacceptable degrees of roughness. For a period of time recently, educators referred to the rough draft as the "sloppy copy." Then we realized that this term was encouraging sloppiness! Sloppy isn't what we want. We want a draft that is legible, fairly well organized, and (after we apply certain criteria) relatively free of basic errors of conventions.

Display your own established criteria on a chart in your classroom as a constant resource for you and your students. As you model daily, you can

This teacher is instructing word patterns that will support students as they spell.

refer to this chart or banner, which we call the Quick Check list, as you clean up your rough draft. (See photo below.) The students can help you with this. We all know that they're much more critical of our work than they are of their own, so this may be an easy task for them! In any case, it will give them good practice daily.

What are the parameters within which you can establish the basic criteria for your class? Here are some tips for you to consider as you make this decision:

1. Remember that these basics are just that—basics. They aren't necessarily the elements that define quality of writing. These are the elements that make the draft easy for the writer to read back and easy for the reader (you or a peer) to navigate. Higher-quality revisions and more thorough editing will come later in the writing process.

2. Choose only those basic elements that you're willing to encourage daily in your own model writing. You'll want the Quick Check list to be truly quick and easy to apply on a daily basis. In the long run, these are the criteria you want your students to internalize and apply automatically every time they write, even beyond your classroom. If your list is endless, it won't become automatic, and it will likely become an arduous daily task for you as well.

3. Pick your battles—a.k.a. your criteria—wisely! If you put an item on your Quick Check list, you'll have to be willing to hold students accountable to it daily—not just in the Writing Workshop time, but in all the draft writing that they complete. To avoid a situation in which you wind up having to remind students needlessly or endlessly, choose only those criteria that are truly essential and doable.

Now, stop and think what you feel is valuable to include in students' daily writing. What are your minimum requirements? List them on paper. We would suggest that you limit your list to between six and ten items. Each item should be so basic that it deserves its very own explicit instruction and mini-lesson. Depending on your particular class and class situation, certain items will be review items for your students (and thus included early in the year) and others will be more sophisticated concepts that can wait a bit. Possible suggestions for your Quick Check list include:

☆ Name and date are on the paper.

☆ Sentences make sense.

☆ Capital letters are used appropriately.

☆ End punctuation is appropriate.

☆ Writing stays on topic.

☆ High-frequency words are spelled correctly.

☆ Resources in the room are used for spelling.

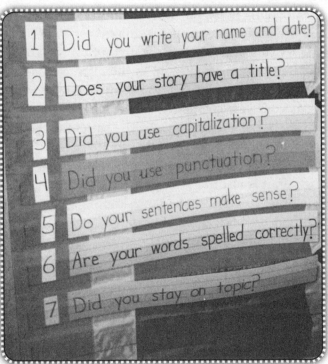

Here is one version of the Quick Check list. This list has only basics that students should remember in their daily writing.

As you teach a mini-lesson and demonstrate a new point several times, add that criterion to your list so that it will be visible in the classroom. You might record each new criterion on a sheet of flip chart paper so you can display one item at a time. Alternately, you might use a pocket chart and add the items on sentence strips. Or, you might be more creative in the display of your criteria. Just be sure that the list is visible and that it's used daily by you and your students. After you display an item, it should become a criterion your students automatically apply. Help students understand that each day the class will spend a brief period of time looking at the list to clean up the writing papers before putting them away for that day.

In the rest of this section, you will find seven mini-lessons to help you get your students refreshed and on their way with the basics.

This student has checked his writing for the basic conventions.

Drafting in acceptable format

EXPLANATION: During second and third grade, students become continually more adept in their ability to write within acceptable formats. They learn to handle the basic writing conventions—such as legibility, correct letter formation, and appropriate spacing—that are part of most state standards. This lesson, a quick review of what is expected, should suffice to refresh their knowledge.

Skill Focus

Writing draft copy in an acceptable format

Materials & Resources

☆ Examples of former students' writing (names removed)

Quick Hints

After removing all names, use work from former students to demonstrate how a piece of writing can be affected by incorrect letter formation, lack of space between words, and general illegibility. Students are usually amazed when they realize how difficult it is to read a draft like this. Let students work with a partner to suggest ways the work could be improved, then have them share their findings with the class.

STEPS

1. Remind students that when they first began to write, they probably used a Popsicle stick or a finger as a "spacer" to help them leave the right amount of space between words. Stress how important it is to continue to space letters and words appropriately.

2. Some students may be still writing in manuscript; others are beginning to learn cursive. In either case, they need to pay attention to correct letter formation. Make sure they understand that even for the first draft, writing legibly is important.

3. Use a transparency to model the incorrect use of spacing and letter formation. Leave room under each sentence for a correct rewrite. For example:

   Mysisteris agoodsoccerpl ayer.
   My sister is a good soccer player.

   S h e g o e s t o p r a c t ice ever y S at ur day.
   She goes to practice every Saturday.

Writing in complete sentences

Skill Focus

Writing in complete sentences; distinguishing between complete and incomplete sentences

Materials & Resources

☆ Sentence strips

☆ Markers

☆ Flashlights

Quick Hints

After performing an experiment, each student might write out (using complete sentences, of course) the directions to that experiment. Or, working in partners, each student can edit another's writing for complete sentences.

STEPS

1. Tell students that the first part of this lesson involves a simple science experiment. After the experiment, you will write a description of it. Explain that your description will intentionally include a few incomplete sentences, which students must identify.

2. Divide the class into groups of three. Now switch on and off an overhead light in your classroom and, if available, a desk lamp. Next give each group a flashlight. Have the groups experiment with what makes the light go on and off.

3. Write the following description on a transparency:

   Electricity is a special kind of energy used to make light shine and machines work. When we turn on a lamp switch, the electricity flows through wires to make it work. The electric current flows along metal inside the wire to the light bulb. An electric socket or battery may also be the source of energy. When the switch is turned off, the circuit is broken and the light goes out. The class a flashlight. a piece of metal at each end. The switch so the light goes on and off. We tried it out!!

4. Give each group several sentence strips and magic markers in two different colors. Ask students to write the incomplete sentences on the strips and to add what is needed in order to make them into complete and meaningful sentences. They should write the incomplete sentences in one marker color and then add words in another color to make the sentences complete. Ask students to identify what was added to make the sentence complete. Remind children that to be complete, a sentence must include someone, some place, or something, as well as an action or state of being.

5. Allow students time to share the complete sentences they wrote on the sentence strips. The three sentence fragments, with an example of a complete sentence for each, are as follows:

   a. The class a flashlight. The class (<u>looked inside</u>) a flashlight.

   b. A piece of metal at each end. (<u>The batteries</u> <u>touch</u>) a piece of metal at each end.

   c. The switch so the light goes on and off. The switch (<u>breaks the circuit</u>) so the light goes on and off.

Ending sentences correctly

EXPLANATION: Second and third graders often use incorrect end-of-sentence punctuation or omit end punctuation altogether. This lesson helps to remind them of the different types of sentences (declarative, interrogative, and exclamatory) and the appropriate ending marks. (See page 96 for a lesson on imperative sentences.)

Skill Focus

Using correct end-of-sentence punctuation

Materials & Resources

☆ Short sample paragraphs

Quick Hints

As you conference with students, ask them to identify the different types of sentences in their writing and to check to see if appropriate end punctuation was used.

STEPS

1. Read to students a short paragraph that contains a variety of sentences. Ask them to listen for statements, questions, and exclamations. (They should be able to distinguish among the three types of sentences before being asked to write them.) A sample paragraph you might read follows.

> Have you ever jumped out of an airplane? Many people enjoy this sport of skydiving every day. It takes skill and lots of nerve to take a leap out of the plane and into the sky. What a thrill it must be!

2. Next, write a brief paragraph with a variety of sentences. Intentionally omit the ending punctuation. Ask the students to help you mark the ends of the sentences correctly. Below is a sample written paragraph. (In the sample, correct punctuation is shown in parentheses. Do not include these punctuation marks when you present the paragraph to students.)

> One day I hope to take dancing lessons(.) It is so much fun to dance and it is also good exercise(.) Maybe I could learn to square dance(.) I have seen this dance on television(.) Have you watched the caller sing out the directions for the dancers(?) Everyone walks in circles and swings in and out of different partners' arms(.) Wow, what fun that must be(!)

3. Ask students to write a paragraph that is at least five sentences long. Remind them to think of sentence variety as they write. They may write on any topic or they may continue with the sample idea and write about something they hope to learn how to do.

Two-Part Lesson: Early Focus on Spelling
Part 1: **Preliminary planning**

EXPLANATION: There are certain words that need to be spelled correctly all the time. We call these No Excuses Words. These words are different from the other, larger category—those words for which best guesses (based on what you've taught about spelling and patterns) are encouraged. Students need model lessons to learn the difference between these two kinds of words.

Skill Focus

Learning correct spellings for frequently-used words (irregular, compound, homophones) and common patterns

Materials & Resources

☆ High-frequency word lists

Quick Hints

Consider creating a spelling file folder for each student. List the letters of the alphabet by either writing directly on the inside of the folder or using slips that you tape within. Under each letter, add the words for which students are accountable in their daily writing. During Writing Workshop, all students can open their file folders and use them as both privacy screens and as resources. Let students enjoy decorating the outsides of the folders.

Preliminary Considerations:

Helping children to understand when guessing is acceptable and when correctness is required takes a good bit of instruction and work on a teacher's part. This first part of this two-part lesson focuses on planning and the aspects to consider prior to modeling the difference between these kinds of words. (The second part of the lesson focuses directly on helping students recognize and remember some of the No Excuses Words.)

STEPS

1. Decide which words are the ones you feel your students need to spell correctly rather than guess. These should be words used with frequency in students' writing at their particular grade level. Many lists are available to help you decide which words might be the most valuable to highlight. Compare these helpful lists to your students' actual writing samples to confirm which words should be addressed.

2. Offer direct instruction about your No Excuses Words during a teaching block focused on word recognition, word exploration, or spelling.

3. Consider creating a word wall, supported by activities to teach and review your selected words daily. Displaying these words where they are easily visible and quickly accessible can be a great aid to young writers.

4. Place visual clues next to homonyms on the word wall to aid writers (i.e., for *right*, use a checkmark and for *write*, a pencil).

5. Include patterns of words as a critical part of your spelling program (rimes such as *-in*, *-ack*, *-ook*, *-ing*, and *-est*). Young writers will learn to rely on these patterns as they spell words.

6. In addition to high-frequency words, it's a good idea to focus on other key words, including contractions, compound words, seasonal words, and content area words. Construct cluster charts illustrating these words (see below), and consider setting less rigid expectations for these kinds of words than for high-frequency words. When students are held highly accountable for too many words, they may not take as many risks in developing their writing vocabulary.

Two-Part Lesson: Early Focus on Spelling

Part 2: **Spelling *no excuses words* correctly**

EXPLANATION: After establishing with students the different categories of spellings—spellings that always need to be correct (No Excuses Words) and spellings that can be guessed—you'll need to repeat lessons like this one often.

Skill Focus

Learning correct spellings for frequently-used words (irregular, compound, homophones) and common patterns

Materials & Resources

☆ Writing sample that includes many frequently-used words

☆ Multicolored transparency pens

Quick Hints

For a fun review of the high-frequency words your students continue to miss, write 10-20 practice words at either end of your chalkboard or dry erase board. Scatter the words and space them apart. Form two teams, line up the teams, and give the first team members in each line a fly swatter. Call out a word listed on the charts. The first student to swat the correct word earns a point for his or her team. Continue until all team members have had a chance. This activity provides an engaging, quick review of words students need to spell correctly.

STEPS

1. Tell students you want them to pay special attention to certain words in a piece of writing that you are going to share with them today. Remind them of the classroom resources that surround them, especially the charts and the word walls. Tell them that they will need to use all of these resources during this lesson.

2. Write the four categories below on the chalkboard and provide an example of each category. Notice that the first category is called "Words We Stretch." These are the special, irregular, difficult, and/or content area words that students are likely to need to stretch or sound out phonetically.

Words We Stretch	Words on Charts	Words on Word Wall	Words from Patterns We've Learned
arkeyologist (archeologist)	notebook	people	found

3. Using the overhead transparency, present a brief piece of writing that includes many of your class's high-frequency words. (You can create or find passages for this purpose, or use the sample illustrated below.) As you read the selection to the class, stop when you reach each underlined phonetic spelling and spell the word correctly.

What People Would Learn from Our Trash

In science we read about what <u>arkeyologists</u> (archeologists) found out about people from their trash. I'm wondering what people could learn about us from what we <u>dispos</u> (dispose) of daily in our school. If they found the tons of pencil shavings that we dump into our trash cans, they would know that we use pencils and that we write a lot daily. If they found the uneaten lunch food and trash, they would know that we don't usually eat all of our <u>vegtabuls</u> (vegetables), and they would know about the <u>utensuls</u> (utensils) we use to eat our food. They would also know that we drink lots of milk from all the cartons. I think they would learn a great deal about our habits!

4. Organize students into cooperative groups. Allow groups approximately 10 minutes to categorize as many of the words in the writing piece as they can. Tell students that each group will earn one point for each word correctly placed in categories. The group with the most points wins.

5. When the time has elapsed, call on each group to list the words from one category. On the transparency, highlight the words in different colors as they are called out. Finally, have each group tally their points.

6. Conclude by reminding students to make regular use of all of the classroom resources that are available as they write each day.

Using spelling strategies for writing fluency

EXPLANATION: This lesson helps students achieve spelling autonomy. When students realize that they can't rely on you for spellings during the Writing Workshop, you will be freer to focus on what is essential and students will have a chance to apply what they've learned about words.

Skill Focus

Using spelling strategies for fluency in the draft stage of writing

Materials & Resources

☆ Spelling Strategies worksheet (Appendix, page 110)

☆ Spelling Strategies handout/chart (to be made from the worksheet: see Step 4)

Quick Hints

Make available to the class a Spelling Strategies chart. (You can easily create this resource for students by simply folding the worksheet and photocopying only the top half.) You might enlarge it and post it as a chart or make an individual photocopy for each child to keep in his or her own folder. Remind students to think about checking this chart when they are doing their own drafting.

STEPS

1. Distribute a copy of the Spelling Strategies worksheet to each student. Note that this worksheet has two parts. The top half includes the five strategies, illustrated in rebus format. The bottom half is a work area for students, formatted in columns.

2. Explain to students, "Today I'm going to show you the different ways that I figure out how to spell words that I want to use in my writing. Look at the top part of your worksheet. It has five spelling strategies that you'll hear me use today. Each time I come to a word I don't know, I'm going to find a strategy on the list that will help me. I want you to see if you know which one I'm using. When I stop on a word, write that word in the column called 'Word.' Then, after I've tried to spell it, I want you to put down the number of the strategy that I used in the column called 'Strategy.' We'll do the first two together."

3. Write the following paragraph on the overhead transparency. Each time you arrive at one of the underlined words, use think-aloud modeling like that shown in parentheses. (The numbers refer to the appropriate spelling strategies from the worksheet.)

   <u>Conserving</u> (*I hear two word parts that I know, con and serve— they will help me. #3*) <u>Resources</u> (*This word is on a chart over in our Publishing Center. I can copy it. #1*)

   The <u>earth</u> (*I've seen this word so many times in our books. I think I can spell it from the picture in my mind. #5*) is <u>good</u> (*This is on our Word Wall. That'll help me. #1*) to us, and we need to be good to the earth. The earth is filled with what we call <u>natural</u> (*I'm going to stretch out the sounds I hear for this one. There are lots of ways to make the /ul/ sound, so I've got to make a guess about the ending. #4*) <u>resources</u> (*Here's the word again that I can copy from our Publishing Center. #1*). <u>Those</u> (*This word's on the Word Wall. #1*) are <u>things</u> (*This word rhymes with sing so I know that pattern. #2*) like water, trees, coal, water and fuel. There are many ways we can be kind to the earth. <u>Recycling</u> (*I know lots of words that have "re" in them, so I can write that. #3 // I've seen cycle many times in our books, and I think I can make a good guess about it. #5*) is one way to be kind. For every ton of paper we recycle, we can save about 17 trees!

4. Make available to the class a Spelling Strategies chart. (You can easily create this resource for students by simply folding the worksheet and photocopying only the top half.) You might enlarge it and post it as a chart or make an individual photocopy for each child to keep in his or her own folder. Remind students to think about checking this chart when they are doing their own drafting.

Two-Part Lesson: Using Classroom Resources for Spelling and Writing

Part 1: **Using the dictionary**

EXPLANATION: In teaching dictionary skills, be sure not to overemphasize correctness at the rough-draft stage. The appropriate time to use the dictionary will be when writing is edited. That's when correctness will count!

Skill Focus

Using classroom resources—a dictionary—for spelling and writing

Materials & Resources

☆ A dictionary usage chart prepared ahead of this lesson (see Step 4)

☆ Age-appropriate dictionaries (as many as necessary)

☆ A well-written sample of your writing

Quick Hints

Creating a resource area in your classroom should be a top priority. You may want it to be a part of your Publishing Center, or it could be a separate area. Include dictionaries, a thesaurus, encyclopedias, and a computer with Internet access, if possible. This area should be always available for students as they write, and using it should be a required step between conferencing and publishing.

STEPS

1. Display on the overhead one of your better writing samples. Explain to students that this is one that you'd like to publish—one that you're proud of and that you want to share with others. Remind the class that when we know our writing will be seen by other people, we work a little harder to get it just right. It is for pieces like this that writers need to be sure their spellings are correct. In draft writing, we sometimes include words we've spelled phonetically. But in writing that we will share with others, we need to change those words into their correct form, into their "book spellings." You might add, "Even our favorite authors do this before they publish their books!"

2. Distribute age-appropriate dictionaries to students.

3. Choose a word from your sample that you had deliberately misspelled during your original modeling (and that you likely circled at the time). Try to choose a word that you had spelled phonetically—such as *pumken* instead of *pumpkin*.

4. Display a dictionary usage chart (see below) as an enlarged wall chart or photocopy and distribute it to each student as a handout. Using this reference, guide students through the four steps as you find your word.

   📖 Think about the **beginning sound** of your word and locate the section that has the beginning letter in the guide words.

   📖 Use the **guide words** on each page to help you find the next letters of the word.

   📖 If you can't find your word, think of **other letters** that could make the sounds in your word.

   📖 When you locate the word, strike through the incorrect spelling and **write the correct spelling** above that word.

5. Using these four steps, work through two or three words together with the class before asking students to use one of their own previous writing samples to try independently to change a "stretched" word into a "book word."

Two-Part Lesson: Using Classroom Resources for Spelling and Writing

Part 2: Using a thesaurus

EXPLANATION: Second and third graders can learn to be discriminating in their choice of words for writing. Because students often struggle to find just the right word, a thesaurus is an appealing resource.

Skill Focus

Using classroom resources—a thesaurus—for spelling and writing

Materials & Resources

☆ An age-appropriate thesaurus (suggested: *Scholastic Children's Thesaurus* by John Bollard)

☆ A previous piece of writing that you have modeled

Quick Hints

Work with your class to make a thesaurus for words they tend to use too often in writing. You'll need these materials for your thesaurus: a three-ring binder, marker, sheet protectors, and paper. On the cover, write "Our Class Thesaurus," so that students will be familiar with the word *thesaurus*. Some frequently overused words that might be added are: *good*, *said*, *nice*, *pretty*, and *bad*. Use guide words to arrange the pages in alphabetical order in the three-ring binder. Putting your pages into sheet protectors will make your thesaurus more durable and help it to stay cleaner.

STEPS

1. Tell students, "Experienced writers know of a special book that helps them find words that will make their writing more interesting. That book has a funny name that sounds a little like a kind of dinosaur! It's called a thesaurus." Write the word *thesaurus* on the overhead or chalkboard.

2. Show students a thesaurus, such as *Scholastic Children's Thesaurus*. Point out its features, including the guide words on each page and the alphabetical arrangement.

3. Write this list for students to see:

   a good student   a good picture
   a good grade   a good thought

4. Tell students that these are subjects that a writer might choose to write about. Have them identify the repeated word in each phrase. Let them know that there are many different ways of saying something—even different ways to say *good*. Point out that when we write, we want to find the most expressive word choices.

5. Use the thesaurus to model how you would find words to replace the word *good*. Strike through the word *good* in each phrase and replace it. After looking up a few of the words yourself, you might pass the thesaurus to a few students to let them help you.

   A ~~good~~ student/well-behaved   A ~~good~~ picture/skillful
   A ~~good~~ grade/superior   A ~~good~~ thought/brilliant

6. Using a piece you've previously written, model reading back over it to demonstrate how you would select better choices for some of the words you've used. Explain to students that there are two times writers might want to use a thesaurus: first, when they're writing and looking for a good word to express what they want to say; and second, when they're reading back over their work and they realize they've overused a particular word or that a more precise word would express the meaning better.

Using the computer to help with spelling

EXPLANATION: Many students have a computer available, either at school or at home, and know how to use word-processing software to write. Students need to be taught that there are spelling resources available that accompany these programs, and they need to learn how to use these resources effectively and appropriately.

Skill Focus

Using electronic resources for spelling

Materials & Resources

☆ Computers

☆ Word-processing software

Quick Hints

Add a little competitive edge to this activity by having each small group tally the total number of spelling errors they find. After the whole class has been exposed to this lesson, reward the winning group with extra computer time.

Have the students electronically compose a letter to their parents explaining how to use software sources for spelling. This will provide additional practice.

STEPS

Note: This lesson is best taught in small groups; you might have the rest of the class participate in the Writing Workshop while you teach each individual group at the computer.

1. Gather four or five students around you at a computer. Display this paragraph (or one like it):

   As sumer winds down, thoughts turn two the start of school, cooler days, apples and pumkins, and leaves turning to glorius crimson and gold. Football games, trips to the mountains, and raking leaves feel the ours.

   (In this paragraph, the following words are misspelled: *summer, to, pumpkins, glorious, fill, hours.*)

2. With this paragraph displayed, walk your students through the spell-check procedures built into your particular software. Spell-check tools vary; just be sure you're familiar with yours before you begin the lesson. Below is a common set of steps:

   a. Highlight the word or the entire sentence to check for errors.

   b. Click on the ✔ ABC icon on the menu bar.

   c. Possible spelling errors will appear in red. (Grammar errors will appear in green.)

   d. Select the correct spelling and click on "change." The correct spelling will automatically appear in the document.

3. Caution students that misspelled homophones may not be identified by the spell-check program. In the sample paragraph, have students find the homophone that the computer did not highlight as a misspelling (*two* for *to*).

4. Also point out that as long as a word is correctly spelled, the computer will not highlight it as a misspelling. Thus, a word could be incorrect in a sentence but not picked out by the computer. In the sample paragraph, have them find two instances of this (*feel* for *fill* and *ours* for *hours*). Tell students, too, that software does not recognize most proper nouns.

5. Discuss the idea that, given the pitfalls just considered, the computer should not be relied on as the sole source for spelling accuracy. It should be seen as a useful tool, but not the only resource for spelling well.

6. After you feel the group has practiced sufficiently with the first sample, display a second piece of writing. This new paragraph should be similar in length to the first, and should include the same number and kinds of errors. Have the group work together to find all the errors in this paragraph.

Planning for Writing

Much of our planning for speaking is done as a mental process. We don't stop to map our words or make a list of the things we might talk about before the words roll from our lips. To phrase it in terms of the writing process, we generally don't do much more than some "mental drafting" before we begin speaking.

Writing in the beginning of the year should occur the same way. As teachers, we need to encourage students to "talk on paper" so that they become fluent and confident in their written communication. For that reason, many lessons in the first two sections of this book emphasize writing about everyday experiences in a conversational way. This is an intentional strategy to set students—especially those who don't see themselves as writers—at ease.

Many teachers believe that their own model pieces should be extraordinary or clever in some way. This is erroneous and, beyond that, it is actually potentially harmful. Without realizing it, we might discourage students with such writing, because it might cause them to think, "I'll never be able to write like my teacher." In our experience, we get students writing sooner when we write about ordinary things in our own lives and when we downplay the preliminary planning elements. There will be enough time later in the year and in subsequent years for students to learn the more technical aspects of planning and writing. Now, early in the year, is the time to encourage their yearning to get going— to just start *writing*.

Our "keep-it-simple" approach to writing continues while we look daily for signs that students are developing confidence. What are the signs we're looking for? We observe their responses as we announce that it's time for the Writing Workshop—do they appear eager or reserved? We notice whether students are distracted during the mini-lesson or really attending to what we're writing. Do they seem to be picking up on the things we're modeling in our writing? When it's the students' turn to write, we look to see whether they hesitate before putting pencils to paper, or whether they're eager to get started with their new ideas. We observe whether they're all too happy to put their work away or whether instead they're excited to share their ideas with others. There are so many signs to look for every day—even the expressions on their faces.

Once students possess confidence in themselves as writers, they usually grow more open to trying new things. They're ready to begin experimenting with styles and types of writing. It's at this point, not before, that we want to stretch them as writers by exposing them to different ways of generating and planning their ideas. This will prove especially important as their writing grows in complexity.

To help students learn to plan their writing, a teacher can make available a whole menu of instructional tools. Within the context of these varied resources, students can make real choices based on their preferences and on the type of writing they are engaged in. In this section, we'll explore:

☆ Different kinds of graphic organizers.

☆ Semantic maps.

☆ Simple numbering and alphabetic outlining systems called for in many standards documents.

Additionally, we suggest that you consult your own state's standards to check whether they require students to use particular methods for performance-based writing tests. If, for instance, you find that there is a graphic organizer highlighted in your testing program, you will want to use it with greater frequency in your modeling. However, even in this case, we would not recommend limiting your modeling exclusively to that organizer. As mentioned earlier, good writers need a range of tools from which to choose. So we need to build a wide menu of choices for our young writers—graphic organizers, semantic maps, story maps, brainstorming, lists, and outlining. Ultimately, after having observed your daily modeling and having experimented with different organizational methods, each student (just like more practiced writers) will decide what works best for him or her.

As students develop increasing confidence, stretch them as writers by connecting them through writing to the content they're studying. Making these connections will help them to process what they're learning and to evaluate it in new and different ways. To accomplish this, your modeling should move from frequent writing about home, family, and personal experiences to writing about science, social studies, health, art, and music topics. In first grade, students' writing springs almost exclusively from the personal, while second and third grades are

These students are using sticky notes in their planning.

transition years. Addressing content areas during the Writing Workshop also helps students to be better prepared to make connections necessary during those subject times.

Above all else, remember that rather than being a laborious and unnecessary part of the process, the planning phase of writing should aid the writer. You'll want to model as many tasks as possible to help your young writers organize their ideas and ultimately their writing. After introducing a menu of tools, allow students to choose the one that's just right for them. When planning is personalized, the writing is more likely to be "just-right" as well!

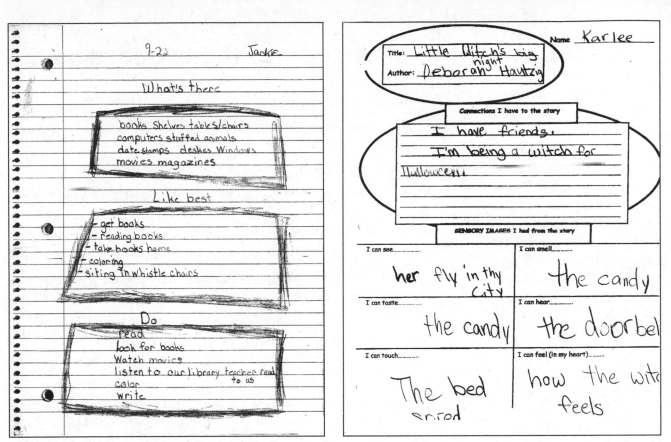

These students are each organizing their thoughts before writing about their selected topics.

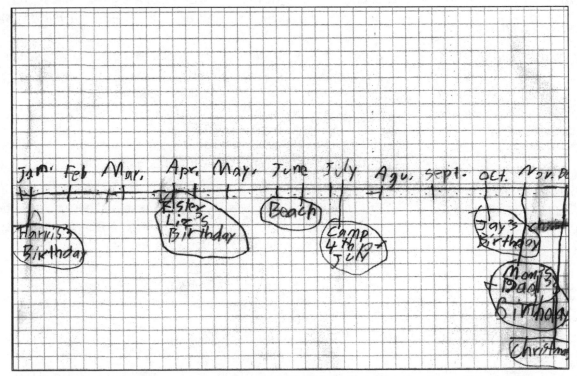

Using another kind of planning organizer, this child has created a timeline of important events in his life about which he can write during the year.

Two-Part Lesson: Finding Ideas for Stories

Part 1: Turning the ordinary into the extraordinary

EXPLANATION: Students will learn to generate their own topics easily once they become aware that there is so much in their daily environment to draw on. Learning to look at their surroundings through a writer's eyes may just take some modeling and urging from you. This lesson uses an analogy to get students to think about their environment in a different way.

Skill Focus

Finding ideas for stories and descriptions in pictures, books, magazines, and textbooks; on the Internet; and in conversations

Materials & Resources

For the simpler version:
☆ A kaleidoscope
☆ Optional books: *Stopping by Woods on a Snowy Evening* by Robert Frost and *Parts* by Tedd Arnold

For the more involved version:
☆ 35mm film containers
☆ Mirrored paper board
☆ Plastic wrap; tape
☆ Small items, such as beads
☆ Kaleidoscope instructions (Appendix, page 111)

Quick Hints

If you've used the second version of the lesson, ask students to write a how-to piece on making kaleidoscopes.

STEPS

Note: This lesson can be presented in either a simple or a more involved version. Both are described here.

The simple version:

1. Show students the simple objects that might go into a kaleidoscope: beads, crayon shavings, colorful pieces of paper, etc. Discuss how ordinary these objects are. Point out that they are of little monetary value and are probably objects that most people would throw away.

2. Tell students that you're going to make these ordinary objects very *extra*ordinary—just by looking at them in a different way.

3. Pass around a kaleidoscope and let each student have a look. As students look through the kaleidoscope, point out that it is constructed from the ordinary kinds of items you have just shown them—glass, beads, and so on.

4. Explain to students that being a good writer involves the ability to take ordinary objects like the crayon shavings and turn them into something extra-ordinary merely by looking at them in a different light.

5. You may also want to share with students several books that illustrate stories written about ordinary events. *Stopping by Woods on a Snowy Evening*, a book based on Robert Frost's famous poem, tells about a man who stops in the woods to look at new-fallen snow. *Parts* by Tedd Arnold is a humorous look at ordinary biological processes like losing hair and flaking skin.

The more involved version:

1. Have each student make a kaleidoscope. Follow the easy directions in the Appendix on page 111 for making kaleidoscopes.

2. Have students try out their kaleidoscopes and discuss how different the ordinary objects now look. Remind them that we often have to look at ordinary things in a different way to find the beauty in them. That's at the heart of good writing!

Two-Part Lesson: Finding Ideas for Stories

Part 2: **Ideas are where we least expect them**

EXPLANATION: This lesson helps students to look through a writer's eyes to see the potential for ideas in everyday materials available in the classroom. It also creates a classroom resource for students, which they can continue to use throughout the school year as they need ideas for writing.

Skill Focus

Finding ideas for stories and descriptions in pictures and books, magazines, and textbooks; on the Internet; and in conversations with others

Materials & Resources

☆ Printed or electronic materials of various types: books, magazines, textbooks, newspaper, the Internet

☆ A sheet of flip-chart paper for each cooperative group

☆ Colored markers

☆ Scissors

☆ Paste

Quick Hints

This lesson can be repeated every few months to help students to reap new ideas from their classroom resources. Eventually, you may wish to have a separate set of charts for each of the different resources that have been explored.

STEPS

1. Remind students about the previous day's lesson, in which they made or explored kaleidoscopes, and ask a few students to sum up what the kaleidoscope taught them about good writers.

2. Hold up for the class some printed material that you've selected—a book, a magazine, or a classroom textbook. Explain that you're going to put on your "kaleidoscope eyes" and look for some good ideas in ordinary things.

3. Thumb through the book slowly, skimming headings, captions, and pictures.

4. Using the overhead, make notes on a transparency about interesting ideas that you discover in the book as you browse through it.

5. Tell students that they will be creating a classroom resource that will help them think of topics to write about throughout the whole year.

6. Arrange the students in cooperative groups. Give each small group a different type of material to comb through for writing ideas. Use a variety of magazines and newspapers; math, science, and other content textbooks; and classroom library books. In addition, you could have one group work at the computer to check Internet sources. Give each group a large sheet of chart paper with the heading, "Writing Ideas I've Gotten From [*fill in the appropriate resource*]."

7. Direct each group to list, to illustrate, or (using material that are disposable, of course) to cut out pictures of ideas they glean from their resources and then to put their ideas on the chart paper. Encourage them to use their imaginations and to expand their thinking to include fictional and informational topics related to what they find.

8. For closure to the Writing Workshop, have groups present their charts to the class and share their good ideas.

9. Hang the charts from a coat hanger with clothespins in the Writing/Publishing Center for students to use as a continual resource.

Ideas from Science

1. life cycles — facts

2. frogs — fantasy story or facts we've learned

3. food chain — try a poem patterned after "There Was an Old Woman Who Swallowed a Fly"

Brainstorming for ideas

EXPLANATION: Many students need support when they're trying to think of writing topics. Brainstorming is one of many techniques that can assist them. This technique requires that students think quickly and say or list ideas that come to mind. Students will improve their brainstorming skills with practice.

Skill Focus

Brainstorming to uncover ideas and information to write about

Materials & Resources

☆ *The All-New Book of Lists for Kids* by Sandra and Harry Choron

Quick Hints

Share with students the book *The All-New Book of Lists for Kids.* This resource will stimulate the technique of brainstorming.

You might think of the activity in this lesson—the listing of categories and subjects—as an ongoing process. Repeat the lesson now and then throughout the year for different topics.

STEPS

1. Together with students, generate categories that will be of interest to second and third graders. Examples might include sports, favorite books, pets, foods, friends, etc.

2. Write one of the categories on the chalkboard or on a transparency.

3. Set a timer for 20 seconds. Ask students to call out any subject they want to write about connected to the category. For example:

   Category/Topic: Sports
   Subjects generated:

Football	Baseball	Softball
Bats and gloves	Exciting games	Soccer
Sports equipment	Basketball	Kickball
Ice skating	Swimming	Canoeing

4. Ask students to construct an individual list of the top five subjects they feel able to write about under the category just brainstormed.

5. Now have them share their lists orally with a partner, perhaps elaborating on or modifying their choices during discussion. All students will then have a list of five subjects that they are most interested in within a certain category.

6. Give each set of partners another category, such as pets. Proceed as you did for the first category, setting a brief time for the class to practice brainstorming.

Warming up for writing

Skill Focus

Planning for writing that includes details

Materials & Resources

☆ Alphabet Chart (See Appendix, page 112)

☆ *Stephanie's Ponytail* by Robert Munsch

Quick Hints

Read aloud one of the students' favorite books and ask the class to think of the plan the author may have used to write the book. Students will undoubtedly have different ideas, so this could become a good class discussion.

STEPS

1. Introduce the book *Stephanie's Ponytail* by Robert Munsch.

2. Tell the students that, as you read the book aloud, they should listen for words or actions that describe Stephanie.

3. After reading, distribute the Alphabet Chart. On a transparency of the graphic organizer, model how *you* plan by filling in a few of the alphabet boxes with words and phrases—alphabetized under the appropriate letter—that describe Stephanie. Explain that these words and phrases become the details that will merge to form a paragraph about the character, Stephanie. Below is an example of a partially filled-in chart.

4. Have students work independently or in pairs to continue filling in words and phrases that will form the details for their paragraph.

TOPIC: Stephanie from Stephanie's Ponytail	A	B bossy	C conniving cunning	D devious
E entertaining	F funny friends who copy	G	H	I
J jumps to conclusions	K	L	M manipulative misbehaves	N nice mom
O ornery	P proud prissy	Q quick to judge	R	S strong selfish smart shrewd
T touchy	U up to tricks unique unfriendly	V	W weird	XYZ

Organizing with letters and numbers

EXPLANATION: Given freedom to experiment, students will learn to organize for writing in the way that suits them best, just as teachers and all writers do. This lesson, with its emphasis on alphabetic and numerical organizational systems, will probably appeal most to the "linear thinkers" in the class.

Skill Focus

Organizing writing into a logical order, including the use of alphabetic and numerical systems

Materials & Resources

☆ Semantic map or web, such as the example on this page

Quick Hints

Stay focused on the fact that this lesson is all about planning writing that is organized. Don't overemphasize upper- and lowercase letters in outlines, and Roman numerals aren't necessary, either. Keep it simple—these are second and third graders!

STEPS

1. Explain that organization is an important element in writing. In this lesson, students will learn to organize their writing using letters of the alphabet and numbers. Using the overhead or chalkboard, present the semantic web or map at the bottom of this lesson.

2. Share with students, "Boys and girls, I want to show you another way of organizing the same information you see in this map. You might choose this new way of organizing your ideas if you want to include a lot of detail. Sometimes if we write more than a word or two in a topic map, it's hard to separate the ideas. I'll show you how to use numbers and letters to organize your thoughts and ideas so that you can include as many words as you want to in your planning."

3. On the semantic map, write *A* next to one of the four subtopics, then *B* next to another, then *C*, and *D*. Tell students that all of the items on a semantic map with a capital letter are equally important ideas; they're all major ideas about the topic.

4. On the map, number with 1 through 3 each of the smaller ideas that connect to the subtopics. Explain that these three smaller ideas are all equally important. They are the details that support each of the major ideas you marked with *A* through *D*. Below is an example with both letters and numbers added.

5. Draw a vertical line to the right of the semantic map and start creating an outline based on the lettered and numbered information. Ask students to help you fill in the outline as you work. Below is an example of an outline.

6. Explain that you have demonstrated two methods of planning in this lesson: a semantic map and an outline. Be sure students understand that, depending on personal preference and on the amount of detail they want to include in a particular piece of writing, they can choose to use either one.

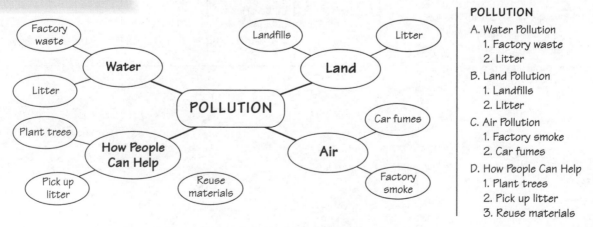

POLLUTION

A. Water Pollution
   1. Factory waste
   2. Litter
B. Land Pollution
   1. Landfills
   2. Litter
C. Air Pollution
   1. Factory smoke
   2. Car fumes
D. How People Can Help
   1. Plant trees
   2. Pick up litter
   3. Reuse materials

Writing questions for investigating

EXPLANATION: Some of your students' best writing will be the writing that stems from their natural curiosity. As second and third graders, they are still filled with unanswered questions about anything and everything. This lesson helps to channel that curiosity into focused questions that they can use to guide their writing.

Skill Focus

Writing and recording questions for investigating; using interrogative sentences

Materials & Resources

☆ Questions for Investigating worksheet (see Appendix, page 113)

Quick Hints

A Questions We Have chart is an easy-to-make and interesting bulletin board for the classroom. This is essentially an open-ended list to which students can add questions they're curious about. It is especially helpful during content studies. The chart also serves as a handy classroom resource: Students can refer to it to choose topics to research and write about.

STEPS

1. Tell students that a good way to get started with informational writing is to brainstorm questions about a topic. Questions can help to guide them as they write and can help to organize several paragraphs into one longer piece.

2. Start to model the process for the class by choosing a topic that will interest your students. For example, if you've had a tornado drill, you might take the opportunity to learn about tornadoes. Begin a list with the heading, "My Questions About Tornadoes," lettering your questions as you write them:

   My Questions About Tornadoes
   a. What causes tornadoes?
   b. Do tornadoes occur everywhere around the world?
   c. What actually causes the damage?
   d. How long do tornadoes last?
   e. How can we protect ourselves at home?

3. Invite students to add their own questions about the topic to your list.

4. After students have added several questions, explain that, while all of the questions are interesting, there are far too many for you to consider as you do your research on tornadoes. In order to write a reasonable paper, you'll need to narrow the questions to the three or four that you're most curious about. Continue modeling by reading back through all of the questions. Explain that you'll delete those that are less appealing to you or that might be too difficult to research. Put the numerals 1, 2, and 3 next to the three questions that most pique your curiosity.

5. Hand out the Questions for Investigating worksheet. Have students use the sheet to create a list of questions about a topic they're interested in. Allow them five to ten minutes to list those questions in the first column. Then give them another five to ten minutes to work with a peer, who should list his or her own questions in the second column. Finally, have each student read over all of the questions on his or her sheet and decide which three or four will be the most worthwhile to explore. Tell students to write those questions in the third column, headed "My Final Questions." Remind them to use the correct form for these final questions, which means including a question mark as appropriate punctuation.

Writing the Draft

Especially in the beginning of the process of learning to write, students find the actual writing—putting pencil to paper—to be the most difficult part of the Writing Workshop. Brainstorming for ideas and planning quickly become second nature, but pulling it all together is far more difficult. Beginning writers confront multiple, overlapping challenges and tasks. Here's just a sampling of questions students must ask themselves as they start to write:

☆ What's the most appropriate title?

☆ Where do I begin on the paper?

☆ Do I need to indent?

☆ What's a good topic sentence?

☆ Do I have sufficient details in this paragraph?

☆ Am I remembering all of the story elements?

☆ Have I created a setting that makes sense?

Synthesizing all that they've learned and putting thoughts together cohesively is a tough job for most students. As their classroom teacher and writing coach, you can make draft writing an easier task for students by implementing the following five guidelines:

1. Continue to reassure students that their priority is getting thoughts on paper, regardless of the correctness of their writing. The only requirement related to correctness is that students use the Quick Check list to check their work at the end of their daily writing. That shouldn't be a tedious exercise; it should become a habit. Remind students that the Quick Check is done so that the next time they return to their writing, it'll be much easier to reconnect to their thoughts because the draft will be cleaner and clearer to work with. Also, if they share this draft as a potential publishing piece, it'll be much easier for you (or a peer) to read and give feedback. The reassurance that you're not looking for a perfect paper will help your young writers to become more fluent.

2. Remind students that they can take as long as they need to write a piece in the Writing Workshop.

With some exceptions, they do not have to meet an end-of-class deadline. It's permissible, even encouraged, to work on a piece for a few days, a week, or longer in the Writing Workshop. Untimed writing tends to relieve the pressure of "writer's block."

3. Create a classroom atmosphere that is conducive to writing. If you treat the Writing Workshop like "office time," where students understand that their daily job is to generate writing, they may be more focused and serious about the work they're expected to generate each day. If you feel comfortable accommodating students' suggestions and preferences, elicit their input about what would help them become productive writers. Make a list of those items on a chart and display it in the room. Here are some points that students might bring up:

   ☆ Rearranging desks so that their privacy is insured.

   ☆ Allowing them to lie on the floor or sit on beanbag chairs while they write in their notebooks.

   ☆ Having them write inside "carrels" created by opened file folders set up on their desks.

   ☆ Including time daily for optional peer meetings to share ideas about writing.

Whenever the Writing Workshop isn't running smoothly, stop and review what the students agreed upon as their working conditions to find out what's not working and why.

4. Expose students regularly to as many samples of writing as possible in a multitude of genres and styles. To be good writers, students need to read a great deal and look at the text through the eyes of a writer. Your daily mini-lessons will allow them to see and hear your writing and sometimes the writing of published authors. And if you build in time at the end of each day's workshop for students to share their work with one another, you'll also expose them to a further source of writing: their peers' work. All of these samples become part of students' writing background and can help them to develop into better writers.

In second and third grades, writing is often connected to content area studies.

5. Finally, offer students praise and encouragement. The praise you offer should be genuine, however. If a student's writing isn't truly well developed, don't say that it is. Students must learn to evaluate their own writing efforts. The criteria you use for what is their "good," "better," and "best" writing will quickly set their own personal standards. There's always something genuinely good that can

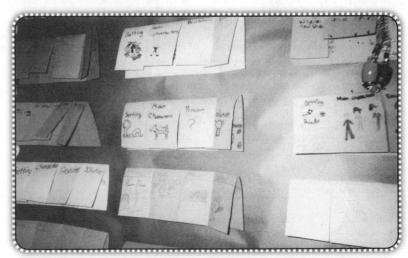

Flip books are used as students plan beginnings, middles, and endings for their stories.

be said about a student's work. Perhaps the writer whose work is not yet well developed put in a great deal of effort or chose a particularly intriguing concept to write about. Applaud these aspects. Keep them motivated!

A student maps the beginning, middle and end of his story across the top as he begins to write.

This enlarged portion of the above sample shows the student's mapping.

Three-Part Lesson: The Beginning, Middle, and End of it All

Part 1: Understanding basic literary elements

EXPLANATION: A complete story is built around a beginning, middle, and end. Stories include the elements of character and setting (introduced in the beginning); plot and problem (developed in the middle); and solution (presented in the end). Through a storyboard, this lesson helps students connect stories they have listened to or read to the stories they write.

Skill Focus

Writing an effective beginning, middle, and end

Materials & Resources

☆ Poster board; markers

☆ A well-structured story

☆ Four sticky notes in three different colors with the following information: (Note that sticky notes b. and c. should be the same color.)
   a. Beginning: Who, When, Where (character and setting)
   b. Middle: What (event)
   c. Middle: What (events) and (problem)
   d. End: Result (solution)

Quick Hints

Make a flip chart by folding paper "hot-dog style" (lengthwise) and then cutting only the top half to form four flaps. Have students write or draw pictures under each flap to tell a story.

STEPS

1. Find a simple, well-structured story to use—one that includes all of the key elements. The story's plot should break easily into the four quadrants of a storyboard. You might select a published story, create one of your own, or use the story provided here.

> It is a beautiful sunny day in a cat's backyard. The cat is playing with a ball. He sniffs and pokes it with his nose. The ball rolls around on the grass.
>
> A strange dog comes into the yard. He barks and runs toward the cat. The dog is interested in playing with the ball.
>
> The cat scoots away because he is afraid of the huge dog with the loud bark. He scurries away so quickly that he leaves the ball in the grass.
>
> The dog sniffs the ball and rolls it through the grass. After watching the dog from behind the tree, the cat quietly creeps back into the yard. As the cat gets closer to the dog, he thinks that it is safe to return. Now they both enjoy playing with the ball.

2. On a large poster board in front of the class, draw the four quadrants of a storyboard (see example below). Place a prepared sticky note in each quadrant, calling attention to what you have written on each note (see Materials & Resources, at left). Put sticky note a. in the first quadrant, b. in the second, and so on.

3. As students watch you, draw a simple picture within each square. Your drawing should depict the basics of the story, with the appropriate structure and elements placed in each square. As you draw, say aloud the elements you are depicting. An example, based on the sample story, follows:

1. Draw the sun in the sky and a cat playing with a ball on the grass. **Beginning: Who, When, Where (character and setting)**	2. Draw a picture of a dog entering the scene and barking. **Middle: What (events)**
3. Draw a picture of the sun in the sky and a ball in the grass with no cat. **Middle: What (events) and (problem)**	4. Draw a picture of the dog and cat playing with the ball. **End: Result (solution)**

Three-Part Lesson: The Beginning, Middle, and End of it All

Parts 2 and 3: **Developing the plot by adding details**

EXPLANATION: The second and third parts of this multi-part lesson help students to elaborate on a skeletal story structure by adding interesting details.

Skill Focus

Writing an effective beginning, middle, and end

Materials & Resources

☆ Poster board from Part 1 of this lesson (page 39)

☆ Paper appropriate for a class book

☆ Markers

Quick Hints

Encourage students to participate in a group retelling of stories read. Students sit or stand in a circle while a prop (such as a feather, microphone, etc.) is passed around. When the prop reaches a student, he or she must retell an appropriate event or detail from the story. In this way, your students rehearse sequence and story elements and have a lot of fun at the same time! This oral practice transfers well into writing activities.

Provide students with a pool of pictures that you have cut out from magazines, newspapers, catalogs, etc. Have them select pictures, order them, and paste them down on a piece of construction paper to create a story with an interesting plot.

PART 2 STEPS

1. Review the illustrations on the storyboard. As you do so, write one paragraph from the story in each square. If you are using the sample story, see Part 1 of this lesson (page 39) for the paragraphs that you might write in each square.

2. Tell students that you now have the "bare bones" of a good story. Explain that, with their help, you are now going to flesh out that story and make it really interesting. To start, ask them, "What would you like to know more about?" Or suggest specific questions for them to consider, such as: Where did the dog come from? Why did the cat come back into the yard? Who owned the cat and the dog? What is a good name for the dog? for the cat?

3. Together with the class, brainstorm possible answers to the questions you posed. Add the elaborating details and new sentences to the storyboard. Below (in italics) are examples that could be added to the sample story:

   It is a beautiful sunny day in a cat's backyard. *Tim let Shadow, the cat, out of the house for some exercise.* Shadow is playing with the ball. He sniffs and pokes the ball with his nose. The ball rolls around on the grass.

   A strange dog comes into the yard. *Rascal belonged to a new family in the neighborhood.* He barks and runs toward the cat. The dog is interested in playing with the ball.

   Shadow scoots away because he is afraid of the huge dog with the loud bark. He scurries away so quickly that he leaves the ball in the grass.

   Rascal sniffs the ball and rolls it through the grass. After watching the dog from behind the tree, *Shadow quietly creeps back into the yard. Tim hears the barking and walks into the yard to see if Shadow is okay.* As the cat gets closer to the dog and he sees Tim, he thinks that it is safe to return. Now *Shadow, Rascal, and Tim* have fun playing with the ball.

PART 3 STEPS

1. Using four separate pages, write the material from each square on a different piece of paper. Have students work in pairs or small groups. Distribute one page each to four of the pairs or small groups and ask them to illustrate that section of the story.

2. Other groups can design a cover and title page. Place the pages in the proper sequence, add the cover and title page, and *voila!* You and your students have a new class book!

Getting focused on a topic

EXPLANATION: Because we encourage beginning writers to "write like they talk," their early writing often reflects an unfocused stream of consciousness. This lesson helps to remind students that writing needs to stay focused on the determined topic.

Skill Focus

Learning to focus on one topic

Materials & Resources

☆ Poster board or chart paper

Quick Hints

Ask students to periodically review a piece of their writing to see if they've stayed on topic with each sentence. Tell them to draw an anchor beside each sentence that reflects the topic.

STEPS

1. Ask students if they know what an anchor is and what purpose it serves for a boat. You might draw an anchor to illustrate for them. Jot down students' comments. A sample drawing and possible comments are below.

   "It's on a boat to hold it still in the water."
   "We have one on our boat, and it's heavy."

   "It's like a weight."
   "It keeps the boat from floating away."

2. Guide the discussion toward the fact that an anchor holds a boat in place and insures that the boat doesn't float away or drift off. Share, too, that there are other types of anchors, but that they all share the general task of holding something in place.

3. Tell students that all of their writing needs to have an anchor to hold it in place. Suggest that they think of their topic as being the anchor. Once writers have decided on a topic, they need to be sure that all of the sentences are connected to that topic or anchor. If a sentence isn't connected, it "floats away" from the piece into another direction.

4. Tell students you will model writing in which your topic is your anchor. Warn them that you might have a "floating" sentence that's not connected to the anchor. They'll need to stay alert to spot it. On poster board, write your title and draw a little anchor beside it. Then write your piece. A sample follows:

   What We Can Do About Bullies ⚓

   Bullies are people who try to frighten or hurt others. We can do certain things to keep people like that from bothering us. We can talk honestly with them and tell them how we feel. We can try to stay away from them or we can run if they try to hurt us. I got hurt once when I fell off of a bicycle. Also, we can ask someone we trust for help or advice. We don't want to do anything to act like bullies.

5. Ask students if there's a sentence that doesn't seem to be connected to the anchor in this piece of writing. Call on a student to come forward and draw a wavy line underneath the sentence that seems to be floating away from the others. (The student should select the fifth sentence in this sample.)

6. As students start writing, remind them to be sure that all of their sentences are anchored!

Beginning with a topic sentence

EXPLANATION: A topic sentence is a convention writers use to help achieve a unified and coherent piece of writing. Often (although not always) the first sentence of the paragraph, it must include a subject (person, place, thing, or idea) and a verb that states the underlying idea of the balance of the paragraph.

Skill Focus

Writing a topic sentence

Materials & Resources

☆ Graphic organizer (see Appendix, page 114)

Quick Hints

Give students a list of vague or obvious topic sentences and have them rewrite them with specific wording. Here are two examples:

Playing ball can be fun.
Rewrite: Kickball is my favorite recess game.

I like to read.
Rewrite: Reading mystery books is a great way to spend the day.

STEPS

1. Tell students that in today's lesson you will write about a scary Halloween experience, paying special attention to your topic sentence. Remind them that the topic sentence in a paragraph usually occurs within the first few sentences and reveals what the remaining sentences in the paragraph will be about.

2. Model for students how to plan a paragraph with a topic sentence by using a think aloud such as the one below. (If you choose a different storyline, be sure that it includes three separate events that combine naturally into a simple topic sentence.)

   Three scary things happened on one Halloween night. If I think about those events first, then I can write a good topic sentence. One event was that my friend wore a costume and a mask with wild eyes and weird teeth. Another event was how we were frightened when someone dressed as Superman jumped out from behind a tree. A third scary event occurred when I turned around and my big brother had disappeared.

   All of the events in my story are about things that happened one scary Halloween night. So my topic sentence needs to give the reader that big idea. Here is a sentence that does that: One dark Halloween night I had a very scary time. Now I can continue writing about the three events.

3. Using a transparency of the following graphic organizer (see Appendix, page 114), fill in each of the three middle circles with an event from your story and then write the topic sentence in or near the top circle. (Note: The version of this graphic organizer in the Appendix includes an additional circle, "Concluding Sentence or Idea." For this lesson, you can simply fold over that part of the page; when you do teach concluding sentences, you can make use of the full organizer.)

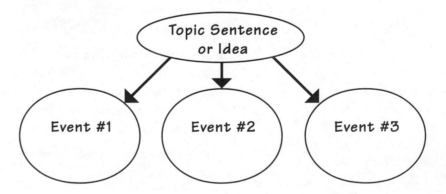

Two-Part Lesson: Grouping Ideas Into a Paragraph
Part I: **Planning the paragraph**

EXPLANATION: As students gain fluency and confidence in their writing, they will be able to understand the use of paragraphs as a key organizational tool. This lesson's paragraph planners graphically demonstrate the elements of a good paragraph and how those elements relate to each other.

Skill Focus

Grouping related ideas to maintain a consistent focus; constructing a single paragraph

Materials & Resources

☆ One sheet of unlined paper per student

☆ One sheet of unlined paper for the teacher

☆ A pair of scissors for each student

Quick Hints

When students are writing stories, they can use this same organizer for their planning by writing essential story elements ("Characters," "Setting," "Plot," "Problems/Solution," and "Theme/Main Idea") on the fingers of the organizer. Underneath each flap, students can make notes about what they might include in their stories.

STEPS

1. Tell students, "Paragraphs are an easy way to group ideas. They make writing easier, and they make reading easier, too! Today I'm going to make a paragraph planner for you, and then you'll have a chance to try making one, too. The planner will have all of the ingredients for a really good paragraph."

2. Explain that the first thing necessary for writers to create a good paragraph is to identify the general topic they're writing about. Now fold a sheet of unlined paper in half from top to bottom (widthwise). Tell students you've decided to write about a science topic for this example. Holding your folded paper like a book with the fold to the left, write on the cover, "Planning My Paragraph on Mining Resources."

3. Tell students, "The next most important ingredient in my paragraph is to decide on a topic sentence that describes the main idea. What is my paragraph all about? I'm going to open my paragraph planner and write 'Topic Sentence' at the top of the left page. Because in our last science lesson we 'mined' raisins out of cookies to learn how real mining is done, I'm going to use that as my main idea. I'll write, 'Mining raisins from cookies taught us many things about how real mining is done.'"

4. Explain that the next ingredient of a good paragraph is to support the main idea with examples or facts. Inform students that writers usually try to have three to five details to support the main ideas in paragraphs. Fewer details mean the paragraph will be weak or uninteresting. Using a pair of scissors, snip the right page into about five sections, as shown in the diagram below. List your details separately on each tab that you've created.

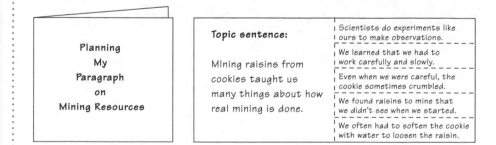

Planning My Paragraph on Mining Resources

Topic sentence:

Mining raisins from cookies taught us many things about how real mining is done.

Scientists do experiments like ours to make observations.

We learned that we had to work carefully and slowly.

Even when we were careful, the cookie sometimes crumbled.

We found raisins to mine that we didn't see when we started.

We often had to soften the cookie with water to loosen the raisin.

5. When you have finished demonstrating your own example, give supplies (paper and scissors) to each student and encourage them to create their own paragraph planners.

Two-Part Lesson: Grouping Ideas Into a Paragraph
Part 2: **Writing the paragraph**

EXPLANATION: This lesson will help students format the notes from their paragraph planners into genuine paragraphs. Students shouldn't be expected to use paragraph planners each time they write a paragraph. However, using them initially can help beginning writers to develop good habits.

Skill Focus

Grouping related ideas to maintain a consistent focus; using a single paragraph; using appropriate paragraph indention

Materials & Resources

☆ Paragraph planners created in Part 1 of the lesson

Quick Hints

Keep a stack of paragraph planners in your Writing Center, already snipped for students to use. You don't need to require that students use these planners each time they write. But having them ready and available will make it easier for those students who could benefit from using them now and then.

STEPS

1. Read through the five ideas on your paragraph planner from Part 1 of this lesson. Think aloud, one by one, about whether each idea supports your topic sentence. If you decide that you won't use one or two of your ideas, fold them under so that you're left with only the relevant details showing on the tabs. Tell the class that it's okay to add words, delete words, or reword in any way they feel is necessary to construct a good paragraph. Students should just keep in mind that everything they include must relate to the topic sentence.

2. Model your decision-making process as you finalize the order of the details for your paragraph. Explain that the point you listed first sounds like a good ending rather than a beginning. Thus, the final numbering for the tabs on your planner will be: 5, 1, 2, 3, and 4.

3. Show students how easy it is to turn the planner into a neatly written, well-planned paragraph. Below is a well-constructed paragraph that results from the planner you created in Part 1 of this lesson:

Our Adventures in Mining Raisins

We tried an experiment mining raisins from cookies to teach us about how real mining is done from the Earth's crust. In our experiment, we found that we had to work carefully and slowly just like real miners do. Even when we were being very careful, our cookies sometimes crumbled, and we're sure that this must happen to miners, too. One solution to that problem was adding water to soften the cookie. We imagine that miners discovered that trick before we did. We were sometimes surprised to find raisins hidden in the cookie that we didn't know were there. We're sure miners must sometimes find similar surprises. We read that scientists actually do experiments like ours to make observations before they perform the real task.

(Adjust the length of your paragraph appropriately for your students.)

4. Read back through your piece and make necessary edits according to the Quick Check you've established for your class.

5. Finally, invite students to turn their own planners into good paragraphs following the same process you demonstrated.

Creating multiple paragraphs

EXPLANATION: Think about how intimidating a page of print would be without any paragraphs! Organizing a piece of writing by paragraphing is an essential tool, one that is often underrated by readers and writers. Paragraphs enable us to read and write in manageable chunks.

Skill Focus

Organizing ideas, including relevant supporting facts and details, into paragraphs or chapters

Materials & Resources

☆ One or two pages of text with paragraphs reproduced on a transparency (suggested text: *If You Lived in Williamsburg in Colonial Times* by Barbara Brenner)

☆ The same text, retyped with no paragraph breaks, on a transparency

Quick Hints

As part of a literacy center in your classroom, provide laminated magazine articles or other interesting texts that have paragraphing. Ask students to use markers to underline topic sentences or to highlight the key words that help to organize each paragraph.

STEPS

1. Ask how many students are responsible for cleaning up their rooms. Mention how you, too, had to do that chore when you were growing up—and still have to do it today! Tell the class that one strategy that helps us to clean up a room faster is to divide the work into parts or categories. When you first look at a messy room, it's overwhelming and you hardly know where to start. Deciding how to organize the work makes it easier to tackle. One possibility is to work in a certain order: first, hang up clothes that belong in the closet; second, fold and put away clothes that belong in drawers; third, put away toys; fourth, make up the bed. Before you know it, the room is clean! Organizing makes a difference.

2. Explain that writing works in this same way: It's so much easier if you organize it. Show students the transparency of the text with no paragraphs. Then, show them the transparency of the same text, reproduced from a book, with normal paragraph breaks.

3. Ask students to consider which they'd rather read. Remark that the uninterrupted solid print version makes a reader tired before he or she even begins to read. It's very much like looking at the messy bedroom—overwhelming! Point out how, in the other version, the author organized the writing into "chunks" or "bundles" that make it easier for us as readers.

4. Bring students' attention to the fact that paragraphs are indented each time they change. Have volunteers come up and circle the "bundles" of print with a colored transparency marker. (If you are using textbooks in which extra space, rather than indenting, is used, you may wish to explicitly point out this exception.)

5. Read aloud the first paragraph and model aloud your thinking about why these particular sentences are bundled together. If there is a good topic sentence that binds them, underline it. If not, just highlight some of the key words that relate to one another.

6. Discuss further with students their own ideas about how paragraphs can help with the writing and reading of their own daily work.

Four-Part Lesson: Using Resource Materials
Part 1: **Taking notes**

EXPLANATION:

Preliminary organization is essential to creating a high-quality, final writing product. Organized note taking assists writers as they focus on what is important about a topic.

Skill Focus

Taking notes from resource material

Materials & Resources

☆ Note cards

☆ Notebook paper

Quick Hints

Keep available sets of large "note cards" that are formatted like traditional note cards but printed on 8 1/2- by 11-inch paper. Young writers will find these visually helpful and easier to work with.

STEPS

1. Tell students that in this four-part lesson they are going to learn how to use sources to gather information about a particular topic. Their own questions about the topic will become the force behind their research. Begin by modeling with a topic of your own choice; our example topic is snakes. On the chalkboard or a transparency, write this prompt: "What I Always Wanted to Know About . . . ." Fill in the word "Snakes."

2. Generate a minimum of three to four questions or one big question with three subquestions. For the example, you might list:

   √ Why do snakes have teeth and fangs?

   √ Why do snakes always seem to be staring?

   √ How do snakes move without legs?

   √ How do baby snakes hatch out of the eggs?

3. Ask students, working individually or in pairs, to brainstorm about their own topics. Each student or pair should write on a piece of paper, "What I Always Wanted to Know About . . ." and complete the sentence with any appropriate topic of their own choosing.

4. Finally, have students develop a set of questions to go with their selected topics.

Four-Part Lesson: Using Resource Materials

Part 2: Taking notes

EXPLANATION:
Preliminary organization is essential to creating a high-quality, final writing product. Organized note taking assists writers as they focus on what is important about a topic. In this lesson, students begin to engage in active note taking.

Skill Focus

Taking notes from resource material

Materials & Resources

☆ Your sample questions from Part 1 of this lesson

☆ Classroom resources: magazines, newspapers, books, textbooks, online sources

☆ Note cards

☆ Notebooks

Quick Hints

To provide extra practice in taking notes, use a T-chart. Label the columns "What's Interesting" and "What's Important" (see example below). Encourage students to use this form when reading nonfiction textbook material.

What's Interesting	What's Important

STEPS

1. Model the note-taking process for students before asking them to take notes themselves. First, display prominently a variety of resources, including books, newspapers, magazines, reference books, and—if available—a classroom computer with online capability. At the beginning of this lesson, you might invite students in small groups to come forward and browse through the resources you have selected and laid out.

2. Using an overhead transparency, model your actual note taking. You might demonstrate how to use both standard three- by five-inch note cards and also a writer's notebook. Especially in the beginning, the larger size notebook paper may be more appropriate for your young students. Show students, as you model, how you do not take notes in complete sentences, but use phrases that contain the key information. Explain that you are sifting out the important information from that which is just interesting. Demonstrate how you abbreviate and use initials as you jot down the notes. You might make your handwriting less neat than usual to illustrate that informality is fine; spelling and punctuation do not have to be perfect at this stage. Point out, too, how you put the information in your own words and do not copy directly from the references.

3. Below is an example of how your notes about snakes might look:

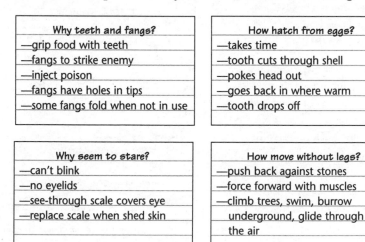

Why teeth and fangs?
—grip food with teeth
—fangs to strike enemy
—inject poison
—fangs have holes in tips
—some fangs fold when not in use

How hatch from eggs?
—takes time
—tooth cuts through shell
—pokes head out
—goes back in where warm
—tooth drops off

Why seem to stare?
—can't blink
—no eyelids
—see-through scale covers eye
—replace scale when shed skin

How move without legs?
—push back against stones
—force forward with muscles
—climb trees, swim, burrow underground, glide through the air

4. Finally, have students begin the note-taking process themselves, using their own questions from Part 1 of this lesson and the classroom resources.

Four-Part Lesson: Using Resource Materials

Part 3: Outlining information from notes

EXPLANATION: Note taking is only a first step in working with resource materials; further organization is needed to make the notes truly useful. Many diverse organizational formats, appealing to various learning styles, are available.

Skill Focus

Outlining information from resource materials

Materials & Resources

☆ Questions and notes from Parts 1 and 2 of this lesson

☆ Pairs of scissors

☆ Tape

☆ Notebook paper

Quick Hints

Provide samples of organizational strategies—including webbing, listing, mapping, and formal and informal outlining—and ask students to file these samples in their writing folders or notebooks. Having these models readily available will remind the students that they have choices in how they organize information.

STEPS

1. It is a good idea to model several of the different formats (webbing, listing, mapping, formal and informal outlining) so that ultimately students can choose the technique that best suits them. In this lesson, the focus is on informal outlining. You can apply the same method to demonstrating other formats.

2. Using a transparency, display your four questions and your notes from Parts 1 and 2 of this lesson. Cut them apart with scissors and think aloud about how the questions should be sequenced. Explain that each question will become an entry on your outline. As you model, demonstrate how your hatching question should come first because that makes logical sense. It can be followed by the other three questions in any order because they do not have a special sequence.

3. Tape the strips on another transparency in the order you have determined. As you place the strips, leave space under each so that you can add your notes. Explain that these notes are really points of information that fit under each entry, or category. Below is an example of how two entries in your outline might look:

Why do snakes have teeth and fangs?

—grip food with teeth

—fangs strike enemy or food

—inject poison

—holes in tips of fangs

—some fangs fold if not being used

How move without legs?

—push back against stones

—force forward with muscles

—climb trees, swim, burrow underground, glide through the air

4. Finally, have students begin the outlining process themselves, using their own questions and notes from Parts 1 and 2 of this lesson.

Four-Part Lesson: Using Resource Materials

Part 4: **Paraphrasing information from the outline**

Skill Focus

Paraphrasing information from the outline

Materials & Resources

☆ Outlines from Part 3 of this lesson

Quick Hints

Extend students' work with the T-chart (see Quick Hints, Part 2 of this lesson) by having students write a summary from the facts listed in the "What's Important" column.

STEPS

1. Explain to students that the information assembled in logical order on their outlines provides the basis for informational paragraphs they can now write. They can combine the new information with their own background knowledge of the topic to write a good paragraph that will answer the questions they posed. Point out, too, that because students took notes in their own words, they will not be copying the original author's work when they write their paragraph. You might use this opportunity to introduce the term "plagiarizing" and discuss how important it is that writers never plagiarize others' work.

2. Using a transparency, model your own writing process as you paraphrase and weave together the points from an entry of your outline (Part 3 of this lesson) into a good paragraph. To underscore the process, do this for two different entries. Point out as you do so that you are now speaking in your own voice, incorporating interesting nouns and verbs as you build a brand-new piece of writing about your topic. Below is an example of the paragraph you might present to the class:

> Teeth and fangs help the snake stay alive. Its sharp teeth help the snake grip a mouse so it can eat the mouse for lunch. If lunch is a bigger animal, like a rabbit, then the snake uses its fangs. As the snake wrestles with the animal, poison comes out of holes in the fang tips and kills the rabbit. Now the snake can eat its dinner. Fangs of the viper fold flat if it isn't using them. Both teeth and fangs play a big part in the snake's survival.

> Snakes have no legs to help them move. However, their strong muscles give them power to push back against rocks and stones and to force their way forward. These muscles allow them to climb trees, to swim through water, to burrow underground, and to glide through the air. With these powers, who needs legs?

3. Finally, have students begin doing their own paraphrasing, using the information on their own outlines (from Part 3 of this lesson).

Giving credit for borrowed information

EXPLANATION: As students begin to do their own research and gather information from a variety of sources, they need to learn how to list those sources so that credit for borrowed information is demonstrated.

Skill Focus

Providing credit for borrowed information by telling or listing sources

Materials & Resources

☆ Sample worksheet for bibliography formats (see Appendix, page 115)

☆ Teacher's and students' resources used in previous lesson

Quick Hints

Make multiple photocopies of the sample worksheet in the Appendix on page 115. Keep these copies readily available for students (for instance, in your classroom library) so that they can easily record information from resources on an ongoing basis.

STEPS

1. Now that students have worked with resources to create their own paragraphs, present a few general rules for writing a bibliography. Below are some basic guidelines. (Note: This list is just a sampling. You may wish to augment it with further explicit information—for instance, about how to list the publisher and the city—or you may wish to simply provide complete sample entries as models for now.)

   √ List resources in alphabetical order by author's last name. If there is no author, then draw a line and alphabetize by the first letter of the title of the resource.

   √ Indent the second line of the bibliography entry. This makes the author's name stand out.

   √ Do not number the entries.

   √ Different kinds of sources require different kinds of information. The Appendix on page 115 provides templates for the key kinds of references.

   √ Place book titles in italics if you are using a computer; underline them if you are writing by hand. Place magazine titles in quotation marks.

2. On a transparency, model for students how to put this information to use by writing bibliography entries for different resources. Use your actual references from the preceding lesson (pages 46–49).

   Book:
   O'Neill, Amanda. *I Wonder Why Snakes Shed Their Skin and Other Questions About Reptiles.* NY: Kingfisher, 1998.

   Magazine:
   Wexo, John Bonnett. "Snakes," *Zoobooks.* (January, 1997): pp. 1–17.

   Online resource:
   _____ *Northeast Florida's Venomous Snakes.* 12/7/2000, <www.pelotes.jea.com/vensnake.htm> (1-25-04).

3. Have students begin to form their own bibliographies by gathering credit information about their own resources (as used in the previous lesson) and following the modeling and samples you have provided.

Two-Part Lesson: Organizing Data Into Useful Formats

Part 1: **Organizing in visual and graphic formats**

EXPLANATION: Written text is not the only means for communicating; graphic aids are essential, especially in nonfiction materials. Students need to learn not only how to read and interpret these visuals, but also how to create them.

Skill Focus

Organizing data, information, and ideas into useful formats (including charts, graphs, illustrations, etc.)

Materials & Resources

☆ Two different pages of informational text (preferably from a content area textbook used by students) on which there are pictures, charts, graphs, and/or illustrations. These pages should be modified per directions in the lesson.

☆ A transparency of one modified page

☆ A photocopy for each student of the other modified page

☆ Sticky notes or a piece of paper

Quick Hints

This lesson can be used as a pre-viewing strategy for any content area reading. Tell students that they'll have just two minutes to take a "visual walk" through the illustrations in a textbook chapter. Then give them a few minutes to list their findings on paper before holding a class discussion.

STEPS

1. As preparation for the lesson, place sticky notes or a piece of paper to cover all of the printed text on your selected textbook pages so that only the pictures, illustrations, and captions are visible. Make a transparency of one of these pages for your modeling. Make photocopies, enough for each child, of the other modified page.

2. Tell students what overall topic is addressed on the textbook page. Using the model transparency, think aloud about all that you can glean from looking at the pictures on a page. Read each caption and think aloud about the connections you can make between the caption, the visual, and the topic. Identify the key words, especially those that tie the illustrations to the topic.

3. After thinking aloud about the pictures, captions, and connections, summarize the ideas in your own words and write that information in the blank space on the page.

4. Distribute to each child a photocopy of the other modified page. Let them work independently or with partners to "read," interpret, and record in the blank space the main ideas conveyed in pictures and captions. Remind them to do the following:

   ☆ Study the illustrations.

   ☆ Make mental connections among the illustrations by asking themselves, "What does this picture have to do with this one?"

   ☆ Make either mental or written notes, using words and phrases.

   ☆ Write in their own words what they've learned.

Two-Part Lesson: Organizing Data Into Useful Formats

Part 2: **Organizing with text and visuals/graphics**

EXPLANATION: Students listen to text that is read aloud, without looking at the accompanying visual aids. They then hear the text again, this time in conjunction with the illustrations, and are challenged to discern what, if any, additional information is provided by these visuals.

Skill Focus

Organizing data, information, and ideas into useful formats (including charts, graphs, illustrations, etc.)

Materials & Resources

☆ A book that illustrates the use of labels, diagrams, charts, and drawings to enhance meaning and clarify understanding (suggested book: *Splish, Splash, Splosh!* by Mick Manning and Brita Granstrom, or any of Gail Gibbons' informational books, such as *The Moon Book*)

☆ Art paper and crayons (for optional, extended lesson)

Quick Hints

Explore all of your content textbooks using this approach.

STEPS

1. You may want to create a classroom display chart or transparency to provide background for a classroom discussion about graphic aids. Refer to the information on the chart (see example below) as you show different pages in the selected book(s).

   The visuals on this page...

   Help me understand better what the author is saying.

   Provide extra information that the author hasn't mentioned in the text.

   Summarize what was said on the page.

   Entertain me.

2. Begin to read the selected book to students. The book you've selected should be short enough so that you can read it comfortably in a fairly short time. Ask the students to imagine pictures in their minds based on what they're hearing.

3. Now go back through the pages one by one to help students focus on the visuals. Reread a whole page and then show the illustrations. With the four points above as guidelines, encourage students to reflect on why they think the pictures are there and to explain their thinking to the class.

4. *Optional extended lesson:* If time allows, or on another day, put students into cooperative groups. Give each group the same paragraph of text. For example, from Gail Gibbons' book, *The Moon Book*, you might use the following paragraph:

   Some night-sky gazers and astronomers can get a close-up view of the moon by looking through telescopes. Some huge telescopes are used at observatories.

5. Tell each group their assignment is to create visuals for the text. Assign each group one guideline from the four points on the chart or transparency (see above); they must meet that criterion in creating the visual. Give them time to consult resources (the Internet, encyclopedias, magazines).

6. Have the groups present their creative visuals to the whole class.

7. Remind students that they may find visuals to be a great help in their own writing, because they can use them to communicate ideas in different ways on paper.

Using organizational features of printed text

EXPLANATION: In their informational text reading, students have already encountered the text features taught in this lesson. In this lesson, students have the opportunity to transfer and apply this knowledge to their own writing.

Skill Focus

Incorporating organizational features of printed text (page numbering, alphabetizing, glossaries, chapter headings, table of contents, indices, and captions) into an original piece of writing

Materials & Resources

☆ Resources and references with information about inventors

☆ Notebook paper; unlined drawing paper

☆ Dividers or construction paper for student-made dividers and for cover

☆ Binding materials, such as staples or yarn

Quick Hints

Keep available samples of books with table of contents, indices, glossaries, etc. Encourage students to work in small groups to look for similarities and differences in the treatment of these organizational features among the books.

STEPS

Note: Although we have not broken this lesson into parts, it should be considered a multi-day lesson. The focus in the first days is the students' report writing; the focus in the latter days is on the assembly of the class book and the incorporation of the text features. Once you get the class going with this project (in perhaps one introductory mini-lesson per lesson phase), you might set up a work center for students to write and assemble as they have time.

1. Start by explaining that together the class is going to create a nonfiction book called, "Our Most Important Inventors." That book will need a number of organizational features that will help readers use it. Review some of the features—table of contents, glossary, captions—that will eventually be needed.

2. As a first step, ask each student to write a one-page report about a famous inventor and to accompany the report with a one-page illustration that depicts the person or invention. Tell students to be sure to provide a caption near the illustration to offer explanation. Some possible inventors they might write about include: Thomas Edison, Ben Franklin, Eli Whitney, Granville T. Woods, Madam C. J. Walker, Alexander Graham Bell, George Eastman, Mary Anderson, Ida Forbes, and Patsy O. Sherman.

3. Group the inventor reports into logical categories. Encourage student ideas for how best to do the categorizing—for instance, they might be grouped according to type of invention (such as scientific, communication, medical, etc.) or by time period. Have students design divider pages to section the categories.

4. Once categories and sequence are established, the next task is numbering the pages and developing the table of contents.

5. Ask each student to select one or two words from his or her report to include in the glossary. (This provides a great reason to use the dictionary to look up good definitions and to make use of the pronunciation key. It's also—for the small group of students still unsure about alphabetizing—excellent practice in that skill.)

6. The next task is the assembly of a simple index consisting mainly of the inventor's names and types of inventions.

7. Finally, invite a group of volunteers to design and create the cover and another group to bind the book together.

8. When it all comes together, your class will have a terrific example of a class informational book that includes important text elements! Perhaps they can share it with other classes, or place it in the school library.

Making Writing Cleaner and Clearer (Conventions)

The research on teaching writing implores us to abandon traditional classroom instruction of grammar, mechanics, usage, and other conventions of writing. A teacher using traditional writing instruction might, for example, follow these steps:

☆ Start with a review of rules and present two isolated sentences with errors that represent abuses of those conventions.

☆ Together with students, correct numerous errors within the two sentences.

The problem with this traditional model is that typically, as students begin their writing, teachers witness the phenomenon of instantaneous amnesia: students make the same errors that moments before they had proclaimed were incorrect!

The research of Hillocks and Smith (1986; 2003) has established that isolated grammar instruction, or what these researchers call *traditional school grammar*, does not result in a higher degree of correctness, nor does it raise the overall quality of student writing. Furthermore, this research reveals that a heavy emphasis on grammar, mechanics, and usage acts to significantly decrease quality writing. Thus, teaching writing conventions—grammar, usage, mechanics—in isolation is not likely to result in transfer from the isolated activity into students' real writing, and it often dampens students' ability to produce a good piece of writing.

On the positive side, research has shown that natural process writing instruction is more effective in developing successful writers, especially as students engage in various writing activities designed to teach them to learn and apply specific writing strategies (Hillocks, 1987). With this in mind, and with a firm belief that getting students to use appropriately what we've taught—to transfer learning to other authentic situations—is the ultimate goal of instruction, we look to the Writing Workshop as a mainstay of instruction.

There are several ingredients in a Writing Workshop that facilitate excellent instruction. The first magic ingredient is *context*. As we model daily for students, we show them not only *how* to apply the conventions, but also *why* we do what we do. Beyond the "how" and "why," we also clearly illustrate for them the power of the application of conventions to our real writing.

We know that underlining pages of subjects and verbs (one line for subjects, two lines for verbs) isn't likely to help students make a connection between that activity and real-world writing. So instead, as we write ourselves, we point out how sentences that express complete thoughts have subjects and verbs. We show students in our own written models that certain verbs are appropriate to use with certain subjects, that certain suffixes on verbs reflect time, and that some verbs are stronger and more expressive than others.

Once students have visible proof how writing can become clearer, more appropriate for their audience, and more expressive and powerful, they'll quickly remember to apply what they've learned. There's a simple reason for this: They really do want to produce quality writing.

Another magical ingredient in the Writing Workshop is *appropriateness*. Both the instruction and the curriculum for a good writing program should take into account what is developmentally appropriate—physically, emotionally, and academically—for students at the designated grade level. A great body of research emphasizes that writing instruction should be consistent with a developmental sequence that recognizes the commonalties of children as they move from early emergent phases to more sophisticated phases (Dyson & Freedman, 2003; Farnan & Dahl, 2003; Hodges, 2003).

The Writing Workshop allows teachers to address students' developmental needs and to teach

> Editing Checklist
> 1. There is a title in the middle.
> 2. Every sentence makes sense.
> 3. Every sentence begins with a capital and ends with a punctuation mark.
> 4. People and place names have capital letters.
> 5. Words that might be misspelled are circled.

Here is one teacher's Editing Checklist, which is displayed on the classroom wall as a permanent resource for students.

A young writer works to self-edit his writing.

students who are at diverse levels of development-Right in writing and literacy achievement in two different ways. First, the mini-lessons address what is deemed appropriate for most students at grade level. However, because not all students are on the same level, the workshop conference time provides an opportunity for teachers to instruct students individually—no matter how weak or strong their writing might be. Teachers must take full advantage of both times (whole-class mini-lessons and individual conferences) for all students to progress with their writing.

We do believe in teaching everything that students need to know about grammar, mechanics, and usage. What we have to be careful *not* to do is to overemphasize correctness during our writing instruction. If we overemphasize correctness, students will quickly get the idea that they can't consider themselves writers until they know all of the things that make writing correct—plural possessives, verb tenses, introductory phrases and clauses, and so many other elements of correctness. Although it certainly plays a part in communicating effectively, correctness isn't what writing is all about.

The lessons in this section share the goal of demonstrating how to teach students what they need to know about correctness in a way that is more effective and more powerful than traditional instruction. The key is in the context, and the context is real writing.

This writer shows that he's aware of basic conventions.

Just-Right Writing Mini-Lessons: Grades 2–3 SCHOLASTIC TEACHING RESOURCES

Using singular and plural common and proper nouns

EXPLANATION: Most standards at the second- and third-grade level address regular forms of nouns. This lesson focuses on the correct use of singular and plural common and proper concrete nouns, as well as the correct use of a or an before a noun.

Skill Focus

Using nouns correctly

Materials & Resources

☆ Wand from a bottle of bubble solution

Quick Hints

Write several sentences in which the proper nouns are not capitalized. Include both singular and plural forms of nouns. Ask students to use a crayon to circle all letters that should be capitalized. Draw a chart with four columns labeled "Singular Common Nouns," "Singular Proper Nouns," "Plural Common Nouns," and "Plural Proper Nouns." Enlist students' help in completing the chart with nouns from the sentences.

STEPS

1. Explain to the class that a noun is the name of a person, place, or thing. A common noun is not capitalized because it does not name a particular person, place, or thing (for instance, *boy, city, day*). A proper noun is the name of a particular person, place, or thing and must be capitalized (for instance, *John, Chicago, Tuesday*). Nouns may be singular (one) or plural (more than one). Tell students that there are a few more important things they need to remember about nouns, including these three important facts:

   ☆ We add an *s* to form the plural of a regular noun.

   ☆ The article *a* is used prior to a noun that begins with a consonant letter (for example, *a picture*).

   ☆ The article *an* is used prior to a noun that begins with a vowel (for example, *an easel*).

2. On a transparency, write a paragraph that includes examples of singular and plural common and proper nouns, some requiring *a* and others requiring *an*. Warn students that, in all of your sentences, you are intentionally misusing the correct noun form and article. Ask them to help you identify the errors. Invite them to make corrections on your transparency by striking out and writing the correction above the error. (Fun tip: Students this age enjoy using a wand from a bottle of bubble solution to point out the errors.) Below is a sample paragraph that you might use for the transparency. (Errors are shown here in boldface.) Following the sample paragraph is a corrected version.

The Election

Last **Week** our city had **a** election for the mayor and town council members. Mr. **rish** was re-elected **Mayor** by only **an** few **vote**. He has been the mayor of **west columbia** for many **year**. The town council race was very close. There was **an** recount of **vote** on **wednesday** and **mr. Teer** won by just three votes! Voters have **a** option of turning out to vote and in this election, every **votes** counted!

Corrected sample paragraph:

The Election

Last week our city had an election for the mayor and town council members. Mr. Rish was re-elected mayor by only a few votes. He has been the mayor of West Columbia for many years. The town council race was very close. There was a recount of votes on Wednesday and Mr. Teer won by just three votes! Voters have an option of turning out to vote and in this election, every vote counted.

Maintaining tense

STEPS

EXPLANATION: Second- and third-grade students need to experiment with using a consistent tense in their writing. As they do, keep in mind that tenses are difficult for students of this age because of the exceptions to the rules and the quirky behavior of so many irregular verbs. Be patient!

Skill Focus

Using verbs (past/present/future) and maintaining consistency of tense

Materials & Resources

☆ Narrative text that offers a good model of tense (suggested: *Dream Wolf* by Paul Goble)

☆ Transparency of one page of the text

☆ Colored transparency pen

Quick Hints

For a follow-up lesson on verb tenses, return to a piece of your own writing. Invite students to help you change the verb tense in the composition to give it a completely and consistently different tense throughout. This is like creating your own time machine!

1. Use *Dream Wolf* (a Native American tale) as a read aloud either during Writing Workshop time or during the block you usually set aside for reading aloud to your class.

2. Discuss and define the term *tense* for your students. Write this definition on the chalkboard:

   tense = the form of a verb that tells the time as past, present, or future

3. After you have read *Dream Wolf* once for enjoyment, together with your students search for clues that indicate the tense this author is using for his story.

4. Using your transparency of the story's first page, elicit students' feedback as you highlight or underline the verbs. Here is the first page with the verbs underlined:

   In the old days people <u>traveled</u> over the plains. They <u>followed</u> the great herds of buffalo.
   Every year when the berries <u>were</u> ripe, they <u>would</u> <u>leave</u> the plains and <u>go</u> up into the hills. They <u>made</u> camp in a valley where the berry bushes <u>grow</u>. Everyone <u>picked</u> great quantities. They <u>mashed</u> the berries into little cakes which they <u>dried</u> in the sun. These they <u>stored</u> in painted bags for the winter.

5. Ask students if they think this author was telling a story about something that happened in the past, about something that is happening right now, or about something that will take place in the future. Remind them that as writers write, they are always thinking about the tense of the verbs they use and about making the verbs show the same time. As part of your discussion, point out clues like the *-ed* ending for past tense. (Note that the first sentence in the second paragraph includes some exceptions that you may not want to emphasize at this point in students' learning.)

6. Extend the lesson with a new example. Write the following paragraph on a transparency for your students. (The paragraph should be completely in the past tense; the underlined verbs are incorrect.)

   Yesterday I went home after school and decided to make some cookies. I <u>take</u> out the ingredients, and <u>mix</u> them together. I dropped the batter on my cookie sheet and <u>bake</u> it for about 10 minutes. They smelled so good that I <u>want</u> to eat one before it <u>is</u> ready.

7. Help students recognize that the verb tenses are mixed up. Work together to make the tense throughout the piece consistent.

Using pronouns as substitutes

EXPLANATION: Learning to identify pronouns is important, but students must go beyond this basic knowledge. This lesson demonstrates how pronouns can help to keep writing from becoming monotonous by giving us different words to use instead of renaming the same nouns over and over again.

Skill Focus

Using pronouns correctly

Materials & Resources

☆ Index cards with one pronoun (*he, she, they, we, it, I, me, us, him, her*) written on each card

☆ Age-appropriate book with at least two or three characters (suggested book: *The Mysterious Tadpole* by Steven Kellogg)

Quick Hints

Keep pronoun use in mind as you model writing, and every now and then point out specific instances of the use of substitute pronouns. You might try drawing lines from the pronoun to the antecedent to demonstrate. Be sure students realize that a substitute pronoun is only used when the antecedent noun is very clear. (If there's even a doubt, assure students that they can simply repeat the noun.)

STEPS

1. Ask students to tell you the word for teachers who come to take the place of regular teachers when they need to be absent. Most students should be able to give the answer—substitutes. Explain that this word means "something that stands in or takes the place of."

2. Tell students that you are going to show them some words that are substitutes. Explain that these words take the place of other words. Hold up the set of index cards you've prepared; pronounce each word along with the class and then hand that card to a volunteer. (Be sure to provide sufficient cards for your activity; in the example below, you will need multiple cards for some of the pronouns.)

3. Read aloud your selected book to the class (you might want to do this as part of this lesson or at an earlier point in the day). Using a transparency, write a paragraph about the book that uses very few pronouns. Read it through with the class. See Step 4 for a sample paragraph you might use. Note that the example in Step 4 includes all the corrections. Your original presentation of the paragraph, in this step, will not reflect those corrections.

4. Comment, "I think this would be better if I didn't repeat the names so many times. Let's see if we can find some substitutes." Start over and strike through the repetitive words. Instruct students to look at their index cards each time you delete a word. If they have a logical substitute on one of their cards, they should raise their hands. (Alert students ahead of time that the same pronoun may show up twice, and that some pronouns may not be used at all for this example.) Write the correct pronouns above the words you've stricken. Below is the corrected paragraph, with words that you should strike through shown in boldface and the correct pronouns in brackets.

Problem Solvers in Our Story

In *The Mysterious Tadpole*, some people were good problem solvers but many were not. The teacher, Mrs. Shelbert, didn't help solve the problem. ~~Mrs. Shelbert~~ [**She**] just told Louis not to bring the animal back to school. The coach at the school ordered Louis to get the animal out of the pool. ~~The coach~~ [**He**] never offered to help ~~Louis~~ [**him**] get ~~the animal~~ [**it**] out. The librarian, Miss Seevers, was a problem solver. Miss Seevers [**She**] heard about Loch Ness lake and had the idea of finding the treasure. Louis was always finding solutions, too. ~~Louis~~ [**He**] found the pool at the school, and ~~Louis~~ [**he**] had the idea of building the pool next door to his house. Our class members liked this book. ~~Our class members~~ [**We**] are glad the problem finally got solved!

5. Reread the whole paragraph to demonstrate how much more fluidly it reads.

Using commas in a series

EXPLANATION: Assisting students in using commas correctly in their writing gives them confidence in trying more sophisticated punctuation. In this lesson, students realize that pausing and inserting a comma between items in a series, and before the words *and* and *or*, helps a sentence make sense.

Skill Focus

Using commas in a series

Materials & Resources

☆ Markers

☆ Sentence strips

Quick Hints

Write a sentence that lists foods to eat. Deliberately choose open compound words (i.e., *hot dog*) so that the use of commas makes a very obvious difference in the meaning. First write the list without commas. Then invite students to help you decide where to place commas to clarify meaning. An example follows:

We like to eat foods like pizza hot dogs corn bread roast beef pound cake chocolate candy and peanut butter.

STEPS

1. Listing any group of items in your classroom can provide the starting point for a lesson about the use of commas. One likely group to use is the multitude of independent reading materials in the classroom. Draw students' attention to these materials and point out that it would be fun to list them in one sentence. Point out that in order for the sentence to make sense, commas must be used.

2. On a transparency, write a sentence such as the example below. As you write, mark each comma with a pen that is colored differently from the text. Name the item as you mark the comma that separates each item. Marking and naming each item and comma reinforces all of the learning modalities.

   The reading materials in our room are library books, magazines, brochures, comic books, TV guides, menus, textbooks, newspapers, and greeting cards.

3. Form groups of four or five students. Assign each group a category (see sample list below), then provide groups with markers and sentence strips. Ask the groups to construct a sentence similar to the example, listing at least three items in a series. Circulate around the room, checking to be sure that students are using commas correctly.

   Possible Categories:
   Things that squeak
   Things that fly
   Things that crawl
   Things that smell
   Things that light up
   Things that are rough
   Things that are smooth

Using quotation marks

EXPLANATION: On the surface, the use of quotation marks seems like an easy skill—open quotation, close quotation. But every piece of dialogue seems to present its own challenge about where commas and end punctuation marks go. This lesson helps students get familiar with several different situations and formats.

Skill Focus

Using quotation marks

Materials & Resources

☆ Age-appropriate book that includes both the use of cartoon-like bubbles for dialogue as well as dialogue within regular narrative text (suggested book: *The Magic School Bus Inside the Earth* by Joanna Cole, in Big Book format)

☆ Transparency created from Appendix, page 116

☆ Marker

Quick Hints

Using a simple storyboard format, encourage students to create original cartoons in which dialogue bubbles are used. For example, if it fits with your health studies, ask students to write cartoon-style ads for an anti-smoking campaign.

STEPS

1. Read aloud *The Magic School Bus Inside the Earth*. First, read it straight through, just for enjoyment. (The Big Book format is excellent for this lesson.)

2. After you have read the book once, select several pages that demonstrate the two different ways that conversation, or dialogue, is handled in this book: 1) dialogue bubbles (without quotation marks), and 2) dialogue within running narrative (with quotation marks). Hold up these pages for the class, pointing out how, despite the different treatment, both types of dialogue reflect the speaker's exact words.

3. Some students may notice that frequently small bubbles lead to a large dialogue bubble. Ask if anyone can guess why the different kinds of bubbles are used. Help students understand that the smaller bubbles indicate that a character is thinking those particular words, rather than speaking them aloud.

4. Select one page that has several characters and dialogue bubbles. (Page 11 is a good example, with four characters talking to each other.) Try to select a page in which the characters' names are apparent; if they are not, just supply some names for this activity. Demonstrate for students how the dialogue within the bubbles could be converted to narrative dialogue; two examples of this are below.

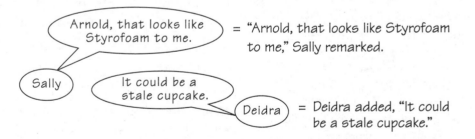

5. Ask students to point out the differences they can detect between the two styles of recording dialogue you've just demonstrated. For example, they might point out where the characters' names are placed.

6. Using the transparency you have prepared (page 116), call on volunteers to help you insert the correct punctuation.

Establishing subject/verb agreement

EXPLANATION: Using verbs correctly can be a challenge, especially for younger writers. This is partly because many rules are not absolute; there are many exceptions and irregularities. Be patient as students experiment with subjects and verbs.

Skill Focus

Making subjects and verbs agree

Materials & Resources

☆ A good/bad list based on a content area topic

Quick Hints

As a follow-up to this lesson, write a paragraph on the chalkboard or chart paper, omitting the verbs. Write verb choices on index cards and pass them out to the students. Challenge students to come forward and correctly fill in the blanks. In addition, be sure to point out the agreement in works that you read or write every now and then.

STEPS

1. A health-related topic can provide interesting subject matter for this activity. Using a transparency, make a list with your students of things that are good for our bodies and things that are harmful. Below is one example, which uses an alternating pattern that helps to hold students' interest.

   That's Good, That's Bad
   Vegetables provide nutrition.
   Cigarettes hurt our lungs.
   A safety helmet protects us.
   Fumes from glue and cleansers destroy brain cells.
   Exercise makes for a healthy body.
   Junk foods clog our arteries.

2. Explain to students that you are going to use this list to check for *verb agreement*. Tell them that this may sound like a complicated term, but it's really something they already do in their everyday speaking. For instance, ask them if they can tell you which sounds right: "The door open" or "The door opens"? How about: "The shoes fits" or "The shoes fit"? *Verb agreement* means that the speaker or writer is using the right *form* of the verb so that it goes with, or matches, a plural or a singular noun or pronoun.

3. Go back through the good/bad list, line-by-line. Have students help you find the subjects and verbs and underline these on your transparency. Read them aloud as you do so, and have the class confirm that these verbs and nouns agree.

Vegetables provide	Cigarettes hurt	Helmet protects
Fumes destroy	Exercise makes	Foods clog

4. Explain that there is a rule for the nouns and verbs on this list: When the subject is a singular noun, the verb ends in *s*. When the subject is a plural noun, the verb does not end in *s*. So for the words on this list, only one—either the verb or the subject—has an *s*.

5. Still working together with the class, change each word pair to test the rule: Make the singular nouns plural, and the plural nouns singular. Read each revised pair of words aloud as you write them.

Cigarette hurts	Helmets protect	Fume destroys
Exercises make	Food clogs	Vegetable provides

6. Briefly explain to students that this rule about verbs ending in *s* does not apply to all verbs and nouns. However, also reassure them that that they don't need to worry about this now. The important thing for this lesson is that they understand that subjects and verbs must be in agreement in our spoken and written language.

Using descriptive words

EXPLANATION: This lesson focuses on adjectives—words that describe nouns or pronouns. Adjectives often answer these questions: Which one? What kind? How many? and How much? You may find that students will voluntarily revise their writing when they see how much fun playing with adjectives can be.

Skill Focus

Using adjectives

Materials & Resources

☆ A sample of each student's writing

Quick Hints

Go on an adjective scavenger hunt. Use multiple texts, including newspapers, magazines, and classroom library books. Ask students to write down the adjectives they find on a piece of paper. Periodically check their lists, and add the most unusual or interesting adjectives to a classroom display chart.

STEPS

1. Define and introduce adjectives, the words that we use to describe nouns and pronouns. Call attention to lists of adjectives posted in the classroom (see Quick Hints) or to other classroom sources, and use these sources as the basis for modeling how to use adjectives. Start with several simple, basic sentences and insert a few interesting adjectives from your various sources to demonstrate how adjectives enliven our writing.

2. Using a transparency, write a simple story. As you write, omit all adjectives. Read your story aloud and comment that you think it sounds pretty plain and boring. Next, rewrite the story by adding adjectives. Go back and circle the describing words you added, and place a dollar sign ($) over each one. Then add up the adjectives circled—with each valued at one dollar—to see how much your story is "worth." Below is a sample story that you might wish to use. The first example shows the "bare bones" version; the second includes the adjectives. (The revised story is worth $10.00.)

   When I was nine, I cracked a bone in my arm. I was skating at a party. All of my friends were there and we were skating in a line holding hands. I was the skater on the end. My skates were zipping along way too fast. Then, before I knew what had happened, my wrist hit the concrete and I was in pain!

   When I was nine, I cracked a ($)tiny bone in my ($)left arm. I was skating at a ($)birthday party. All of my ($)best friends were there and we were skating in a ($)straight line holding hands. I was the ($)nervous skater on the end. My ($)speedy skates were zipping along way too fast. Then, before I knew what had happened, my ($)fragile wrist hit the ($)rough concrete and I was in ($)extreme pain!

3. Ask students to select a piece of their own writing that they think could use some enlivening. Tell them to go back through it to see how many adjectives they can add. Have them circle these words and put dollar signs over each one. (You may want to help students to first underline the nouns; this makes deciding where to add the adjectives a much easier task.) Invite students to total up their dollars and to share with the class how much their story is worth. This lesson helps them practice their math skills, too!

Learning when to use apostrophes

Skill Focus

Using apostrophes in contractions and possessives

Materials & Resources

☆ Markers in two colors

☆ Two blank poster-size, two-column charts

Quick Hints

Check for correct use of apostrophes during individual writing conferences. Students may attempt to use forms of contractions and possessives that you have not taught explicitly, and which are not addressed in second- and third-grade level standards. This is fine; individual conferencing is the ideal time to encourage students to stretch their writing skills.

STEPS

1. On a transparency, write a paragraph-length story that focuses on apostrophe use. Tell students that this story will help them better understand how to use this punctuation mark correctly in a piece of writing. Below is a sample paragraph.

Going Fishing

Have you ever gone fishing on a warm spring day? James, Kevin, and I decided to go on a Saturday in April. We found the perfect fishing hole and took our poles and bait. Kevin dug up worms for bait with his daddy's shovel. James tied the line and hook on each pole so we'd be ready for action. We couldn't believe how the day's catch added up! Not two, not four, not six, but eight large bass ended up in our bucket! My pole's line was almost worn through from the weight of the fish. We weren't surprised to see that all of the bait was gone. James shouted, "It's time to head home and cook our fish for dinner!" That Saturday in April will be one to remember.

2. After you have finished writing, read the story aloud. Then go back through it line by line. Underline the contractions in red and the possessives in green.

3. Call attention to the two poster-size, two-column charts that you prepared in advance (either on chart paper or on the chalkboard). Divide the class into two groups. Instruct one group that their job is to write all of the story's contractions in the chart, and tell the other group that they are to list all the possessives. The first group should write the two words the contraction stands for in addition to writing the contraction itself. Along with the possessive, the second group should list what belongs to what or to whom. In order to insure that as many children as possible get a chance to fill in the chart, you might have one student fill in the contraction and another fill in the two words in the contraction. Below are two sample charts, with the correct entries filled in.

Contractions	Words in the contraction
we'd	we would
couldn't	could not
weren't	were not
it's*	it is

Possessives	What belongs to what or whom
Daddy's	shovel belongs to daddy
day's	catch belongs to the day
pole's	line belongs to the pole

*Explain to students that *it's* is a special case. Only the contraction uses an apostrophe; the possessive *its* does not use an apostrophe.

Capitalizing words

EXPLANATION: Students have likely been introduced to the basics of capitalization. In this lesson, students apply their observation and deductive reasoning skills as they reflect on when and why they need capital letters in their writing.

Skill Focus

Capitalizing words at the beginnings of sentences and using them for proper nouns, geographical names, holidays, historical periods, and special events (see also lesson on letters and envelopes, page 86, for further capitalization skills)

Materials & Resources

☆ Textbooks from several different content areas

☆ Classroom library books

☆ A prepared transparency, listing categories/reasons for capitalization

Quick Hints

When this lesson's list is complete, you might photocopy it and give a copy to each student to keep in his or her writing folder. You might also make it into a classroom display chart to hang in the room, and/or use it as a reference sheet in the resource area of the Writing Center.

STEPS

1. Tell students that this lesson explores the many different uses of capital letters in our writing, and that they are going to create a list of reasons for using capital letters.

2. Organize students into small groups. Explain that each group will generate a list of the different reasons for using capital letters by looking through classroom resources for examples. You can make this competitive if you like, letting groups earn points for the number of reasons they list.

3. Instruct each group to appoint a secretary whose job is to record the list of reasons. Make available to the groups as many resources as possible, including content area textbooks and classroom library books.

4. Show students how to get started by modeling your own list of examples from a classroom book. For instance, you might title your list and include the two categories shown below. Thumb through the book and fill in a few entries for each of your two categories.

When We Should Use Capital Letters
People's names
To start a sentence

5. Make sure students realize that they don't have to read all of the text they're reviewing—in fact, suggest that the best strategy is just skimming the pages for uppercase letters. When students find an example, they should explain to the rest of their group why the capital letter is used in that instance. If they have trouble deciding on a reason, they should simply copy down the example so that the class can discuss it later.

6. Set a time limit for the capital letter search, then ask students to get started. When time is up, display a prepared transparency that you've titled, "Reasons for Using Capital Letters." Your transparency should include two or three reasons as samples. On a rotating basis, invite each group to add one of their reasons to this list. Clarify any misunderstandings the group might have as you record their information. (Depending on how much time the groups need, you might do this step either during the same Writing Workshop or on the following day.) Following is a set of categories that the final list might include:

beginnings of sentences	special events
proper nouns	historical periods
geographical names (states, cities, counties,...)	months and days of the week
holidays	titles and initials of people

Making Writing Better (Revision)

Think about a really good book you've read lately—one that you couldn't put down, one that you missed after you'd finished it. Now, take a minute to think about what made that book memorable. Was it a character who was so well written that he or she became a friend? Was it the vivid description of the scenery that let you escape momentarily to join an adventure? Or was it perhaps the intrigue of the plot or the surprise ending?

If you were to actually make a list of the top three reasons you enjoyed the book, we're willing to bet some writing elements would not be among those on your list. Did you love it because the sentences were all complete? Did it make you read well into the night because the writer always remembered to use commas in a series of adjectives? Or was it because the subjects and verbs all agreed?

Admittedly, if the book had been riddled with errors, you might not have enjoyed it the way you did, because you would have been distracted from the other elements of quality writing. Conventions facilitate reading and understanding; however, they are only a fraction of what good writing is all about. Unfortunately, for far too long in our schools, conventions received a disproportionate amount of instructional time, causing students to assume that writing was all about correctness. Consequently, many students chose to play it safe and write nice, clean—and, well, boring—compositions. A piece of writing that is perfect in terms of conventions might not be a good piece of writing at all.

We believe that in the Writing Workshop classroom, teachers need to dispel the notion that correctness is what it's all about. We let our students know that correctness counts, but that many other elements also count in producing quality writing.

Once writers have completed a draft and glimpsed some potential there, they should want to work with it further. That is the time to cut and paste, mold and polish, reword and rewrite. Only during this revision work will writers discover their diamond in the rough—a genuinely good piece of writing well worth the time and effort spent. Editing for correctness makes our work cleaner and easier to read, but only real revising gives it quality and makes it a pleasure to read. This section presents a set of lessons to help students accomplish that goal.

The word wall in this classroom helps writers to make good word choices.

Students are supported by specialized vocabulary in their environment.

Using sequencing and time order words

EXPLANATION: Young writers often write stories that include events that occurred in their own lives. The concept of sequencing these events logically needs to be learned. Time order words such as *first, before, next,* and *late*—all of which show the order of events—are very helpful.

Skill Focus

Using logical progression and sequence and employing transitional words, phrases, and sentences

Materials & Resources

☆ Sequencing chart, made into a transparency (see Appendix, page 117)

Quick Hints

Have students read stories that include a series of events. Ask them to retell the events in order to a partner. Then invite them to illustrate these events in comic strip format.

STEPS

1. Explain to students that you are going to focus on how writers order events in their stories and compositions. Without order, or sequence, a story wouldn't make sense and readers would get confused. Using a transparency, model writing your own story first. It should be a story that includes a particular series of events. Think aloud about the order of the events as you do your model writing. Below is a sample paragraph that you might use:

A Special Badge

As a Girl Scout, I loved to earn badges to wear on my uniform. To earn a badge, one of the activities I took part in was visiting an elderly lady who spent long days alone. Before making the visit, I would make cookies, arrange flowers, or practice a song. Then I would surprise the lady by presenting her one of my creations. Next, we would look at her family photos so she could recall happy times. Later, we would take a walk and plan my next visit. Earning this badge was fun for me.

2. Go back through the story and call on volunteers to help you identify the clues to sequence (time order words). Insert the clue words into the left side of the sequencing chart (Appendix, page 117). Again with help from the class, list the events in order on the right side of the chart. A completed chart is below:

Clue Words	Events
Before	Make cookies, arrange flowers, etc.
Then	Present creation to the lady
Next	Look at family photos
Later	Take a walk

3. In their daily writing, as the students write stories that include important events in their lives, remind them to list these events in a logical order and to use time order words as clues for the reader.

Using imagery in writing

EXPLANATION: When students experiment with language, the result is usually a piece of writing that is descriptive and entertaining. Developing writers come to realize that, by using imagery, they can help their readers to form pictures of the events and people they are describing.

STEPS

1. With the exception of similes and metaphors, students should be familiar by now with most of the forms of language emphasized in this lesson. Explain to students that *similes* are the comparison of two unlike things in which a word of comparison (*as* or *like*) is used. Metaphors also compare two unlike things but no word of comparison is used. One thing is just said to *be* another thing. (Note that for most students metaphors are more challenging to grasp because they are less concrete than similes.)

2. Demonstrate the use of imagery by writing a descriptive piece on a transparency. As you write, explicitly point out the descriptive language used to help the reader visualize. Include at least one example of each of these categories: adjectives, adverbs, action verbs, sensory details, similes, and metaphors. A sample paragraph is provided below. If you choose to write your own paragraph, it is a good idea to focus on a recent event at school, which students might be able to recall vividly.

The Class Musical

The students in Mrs. Zion's third-grade class came to life last night. Their rendition of "The Mouse Who Lost Its Squeak" was as smooth as silk. The students danced like wind-up toys as they scooted and flitted across the stage. Their voices flowed like thick, sweet honey. As the loss of the squeak was portrayed, the mouse, played by Emily Floyd, was a shining star. Tim Gilroy's lion voice roared thunderously as he scared the timid mouse in the jungle. The musical cast, directed by Mrs. Wise, made sounds like orchestra instruments as the jungle animals went on stage. From my front-row seat, the gleaming presentation was a colossal success.

3. Distribute photocopies of the Imagery Chart (Appendix, page 118) to students. Ask them to work individually or in pairs to look for examples of words in your story that fit the chart classifications. See below for a completed chart for the first six images:

Imagery Language	Classification
came to life last night	Sensory detail
as smooth as silk	Simile
like wind-up toys	Simile
scooted and flitted	Action verbs
like thick, sweet honey	Simile
was a shining star	Metaphor

Skill Focus

Creating imagery by using adjectives, adverbs, similes and metaphors, sensory details, and /or concrete examples.

Materials & Resources

☆ Photocopies for the class of the Imagery Chart (see Appendix page 118)

Quick Hints

Read aloud many books that contain figurative language. Focus on how these language techniques help readers visualize a story's events. Invite students to search for examples of imagery in their independent reading and to record these examples in their writing notebooks or perhaps on a classroom display chart.

Three-Part Lesson: Learning From Authors

Part 1: **Using others' ideas as models**

EXPLANATION: Although your own writing models are invaluable, it's not wise to limit your students to just these pieces. Published authors make wonderful "co-teachers." In this lesson, the models are ideas from a book that (we predict) will be a springboard for lots of new student writing!

Skill Focus

Using literary models to develop and refine writing

Materials & Resources

☆ Recommended book: *The All-New Book of Lists for Kids* by Sandra and Harry Choron

Quick Hints

Make a class book of lists by having all students contribute a list they've written. You might suggest that they write one silly list ("10 Excuses for Not Having Your Homework," "8 Ways to Hide an Elephant," "5 Kinds of Sandwiches You Wouldn't Want to Eat," etc.) and one based on an area of their expertise ("How to Take Care of a Gerbil," "5 Ways to Make a Friend," "10 Ways to Say I'm Sorry", etc.).

STEPS

1. *The All-New Book of Lists for Kids* is a source of wonderful, kid-captivating lists to read aloud to your students either during Writing Workshop or during your normal read-aloud time. Below is a sampling of some of these intriguing lists:

   • *9 Famous People Who Had Health Problems When They Were Kids*

   • *10 Tips for Looking Good in Your School Picture*

   • *The 10 Worst Things About Having a Younger Brother or Sister*

   • *The 8 Best Things About Being an Only Child*

   • *8 Skateboard Safety Tips*

   • *8 Mistakes in Willy Wonka and the Chocolate Factory*

2. Tell students, "Even though we've often made brainstorming lists before writing, many of you may not have thought of lists as being good writing pieces. Today we're going to try to write a list together. The numbering will make organizing this kind of writing very easy for us! Let's try to take one of the topics we read about and turn it around a bit. Instead of writing '10 Tips for Looking Good in Your School Picture,' let's change it to '10 Things to Guarantee You Look Your Worst on School Picture Day.' This should be fun!"

3. Encourage students to think up some off-beat tips for this topic. Following are a few suggested by children in our own classrooms:

   5 Things to Guarantee You Look Your Worst on School Picture Day

   • Don't brush your hair that morning.

   • Don't brush your teeth that morning.

   • Wear clothes that don't match.

   • Take a bite of your peanut butter sandwich before you have to smile.

   • Say "French fries" instead of "cheese" when they snap the picture.

4. In addition to encouraging students to simply have fun creating imaginative lists, one of this lesson's goals is to keep students on the lookout in books they read for new ideas that might inspire different kinds of writing. So be sure to remind them to do just that in their independent reading.

Three-Part Lesson: Learning From Authors

Part 2: **Using text structure models**

EXPLANATION: Second- and third-grade students are already familiar with a number of text structures. As social studies becomes a greater part of the curriculum, it is appropriate to introduce the additional text structures of journals, diaries, and memoirs—the focus of this lesson.

Skill Focus

Using literary models to develop and refine writing

Materials & Resources

☆ Diary literary models, including these recommended books:
Catherine, Called Birdy by Karen Cushman
Dear Mr. Henshaw by Beverly Cleary
Emma's Journal: The Story of a Colonial Girl by Marissa Moss
Rachel's Journal: The Story of a Pioneer Girl by Marissa Moss

Quick Hints

Keep a classroom diary. Each day, circulate a composition book to a different student; that student's job is to enter the class news of the day. Be sure students remember to date each entry. Keep the classroom diary in an accessible place, such as in a literacy center. Don't be surprised if reading the classroom diary becomes one of the students' favorite activities during independent reading time!

STEPS

1. Prior to the beginning of this lesson, make available to the class model texts written in diary form (those listed in Materials & Resources are recommended). You might read aloud one or more of these books or assign them to students as independent reading.

2. Explain to students that, when an author wishes to tell a story through chronological events, a diary format works well. Tell students, "Marissa Moss, author of *Emma's Journal*, wanted to tell the story of events of the American Revolution through the eyes of a 10-year-old girl. These journal entries are written in first person, as if Emma is talking to us."

3. Tell students to "listen in" as you relate events from a special person's life. You will be describing these events as if you were that person yourself, and you'll do this by writing first-person diary entries in a journal. You might explain it this way: "I am going to pretend to be a tennis star and tell you about some events leading to the tournament at Wimbledon. The first entry could be about my practice session, and next I might tell about my workout, diet, etc. This is what the diary entries would look like in writing." Using a transparency, write several model diary entries. A sample follows:

   September 3, 2004
   I woke up early to start practice before the heat of the day. My friend, Karen, met me at the practice court and we played three sets of tennis. I thought I played well, but she won 6-4, 3-6, and 6-2.

   September 4, 2004
   I decide to eat lots of energy-building food so I won't get tired playing. About 10:00 a.m., I went to Kroger's and bought apples, bananas, and grapes. I also chose three kinds of pasta.

4. Next, have students create their own diary entries. You might say, "Think of the published diaries that we all read earlier this week. Think about the models we just looked at in class. Let's use this diary writing idea in our own writing today. Jason, you might write diary entries for a star baseball player since that is your favorite sport. Anna, you want to be a veterinarian so your diary entries could include a typical week in a veterinarian's office. Madison, you read Paul Revere's biography, could you write diary entries that represent this special time in history?"

5. Encourage students to share their diary entries.

Three-Part Lesson: Learning From Authors

Part 3: Using organization models

EXPLANATION: Many texts are organized with a clear beginning, middle, and ending. Second and third graders need to be familiar with this basic organizational structure—both as readers and as writers.

Skill Focus

Using literary models to develop and refine writing

Materials & Resources

☆ Age-appropriate text, both books and shorter pieces, that are built around beginning, middle, and ending text structure (used in this lesson: *The Magic School Bus Inside the Human Body* by Joanna Cole)

Quick Hints

Encourage students to include a section on various text structures in their writing notebooks. They should create a chart like the following, with titles in one column and writing structures in the other.

Book Title	Text Structure
If You Give a Mouse a Cookie by Laura Numeroff	Circular
Suddenly by Colin McNaughton	Repeating Words

STEPS

1. Review with students the frequently-used text structure of beginning, middle, and ending. (See Section 3, pages 36–40 for related lessons.)

2. Next introduce *The Magic School Bus Inside the Human Body* by Joanna Cole. Tell students that this book is a good example of this text structure and that you want them to listen hard for clues that tell readers about the organization. Read the book aloud, pausing as you do to identify the beginning, middle, and ending, as well as to point out key transitional words. Focus on these three sentences:

   Beginning: "It all began when Ms. Frizzle showed our class a filmstrip about the human body." (p. 4)

   Middle: "We were swept out of the bus and into the bloodstream." (p. 19)

   Ending: "At last, everything was quiet in Ms. Frizzle's class—everything, of course, except her dress!" (p. 37)

3. To further reinforce what students have now experienced in a published author's work, use a transparency to model writing a brief story with this same structure. You might use the example below. Work with students to figure out the transitions among the sections. Add slash marks to separate them as you and the class make your decisions. (The example below includes two sets of boldfaced double slashes that indicate the correct spots.)

   ### The Accident

   The day began as I got ready to go to school. I had to bundle up my daughter, Melissa, and make sure she was safely buckled in her infant seat. I knew that the trip to the babysitter's house would take about 15 minutes. I left my house with enough time to get there. **//** As I turned into the babysitter's driveway, a speeding truck hit our car in the left rear bumper! There was a loud crash and then Melissa started to cry. I was really scared, but I jumped out of the car and quickly released her from the car seat. We were safe, but dazed. **//** About two hours later, I was finally able to head off to school.

3. As part of this lesson or their next writing assignment, have students write about an event in their lives and to include a clear beginning, middle, and ending based on the models they have experienced.

Collecting interesting words

EXPLANATION: Students need to learn that the English language offers countless words to express feelings, thoughts, and ideas. There are so many choices that thoughtful writers can find "just-right" words that connote precisely what they want to say.

Skill Focus

Choosing vocabulary that communicates clearly and concisely; collecting words for use in writing

Materials & Resources

☆ A book that illustrates clear, concise word choice (used in this lesson: *Moonflute* by Audrey and Don Wood)

☆ A section of students' writing folders, or folders made specifically for this purpose

☆ Sticky notes

Quick Hints

Here's how to make a handy notebook for students to record their collected words: Take a marble composition book with sewn binding and have it cut in half widthwise. (A print shop can do this, or your local hardware store or high school machine shop may have a fine blade saw that can also do the job well.) Place either a mailing label or an inexpensive, decorative self-adhesive nametag on the cover to allow space for a prominent, personal title.

STEPS

1. Discuss the concept of exciting, just-right words with students. Say something like, "As writers, we should always be observant. We should always be looking for a possible story or even for interesting characters' names. We should also look for interesting words or more expressive ways of saying what we want to say."

2. Read aloud a story or other text to your students. As you read, comment on certain interesting word choices and place sticky notes on them. Following are comments that you might make while reading *Moonflute*, a beautifully descriptive and illustrated picture book by Audrey and Don Wood. (If you decide to use a different or additional book, just be sure to select one that demonstrates clear, concise word choices and interesting vocabulary.)

   "Listen to these adjectives the authors use on one page to describe the light of the moon: it *quivered* and *glowed*, *startling brightness*, *moon-treasure* (I like the hyphenated word they created here!), and a *sliver of light*." (p. 4)

   "Here's a way I wouldn't have thought of to describe music: It *trickled like water over rocks*, *clinked like crystal chimes in the wind*, and *jingled like brass bells on a sleigh*. That's a pretty musical line because of the words!" (p. 6)

   You might sum up your overall reaction by saying something like, "This book is filled with great choices of expressive verbs and descriptive adjectives!"

3. Remind students that independent reading time is an excellent time to gather new words that express thoughts and feelings differently. Students can jot down these ideas in their regular writer's notebooks or in their special journals (see optional fifth step below and this lesson's Quick Hints). They can then keep their notebooks or journals handy and use them for reference as they write their own stories and compositions.

4. Periodically, invite students to share their new word discoveries with the rest of the class.

5. ***Optional step:*** Tell students that you have a new journal for them that will help them to become better writers. Distribute the notebooks described in Quick Hints. Have students use these ~ dedicated new-word journals for the remainder of the sc~

Working with specialized vocabulary

Skill Focus

Using specialized vocabulary in writing

Materials & Resources

☆ New specialized vocabulary words from content area studies

☆ Background information from cinquain poem lessons, Section 6, pages 91–92

Quick Hints

As a modification of this lesson, have students take a sheet of paper and fold it twice, creating four small sections (or fold it in half three times to create eight smaller sections). On each small section, have students add their new words and illustrate them to demonstrate understanding. ...they might fill a ...illustr original booklet w... This

74

STEPS

1. As preparation for this lesson, read through the cinquain lessons in Section 6, pages 91–92. You may wish to teach those two lessons before asking students to attempt this one. (Remember, the sequence of most of these lessons is very flexible.)

2. Tell students that the purpose of today's lesson is to help them use and better remember special new words from a science (or social studies) unit that they've studied recently, and at the same time to have some fun writing a poem. In today's lesson, they will be writing cinquain poems, with certain modifications to help them focus on special vocabulary. Explain that, instead of using just any adjectives in the second lines of their poems, they will need to think of adjectives that specifically describe the selected science or social studies subject. They will also need to make the fourth line focus directly on the topic and answer an informational question. (Help them out with this line by giving direction such as, "On this line, tell how this is useful.")

3. On a transparency, model writing a subject-based cinquain poem. Below is an example incorporating new words from a soil conservation unit, which the class working with this model had recently studied.

Loam	(state the subject)
Rich, nutritious	(2 words that tell more about the subject)
Enriching, growing, fertilizing	(3 "ing" words about what the subject does)
Humus makes plants grow.	(sentence about its usefulness)
Topsoil	(synonym of the subject)

4. Give students the opportunity to write their own cinquain poems to show their knowledge of specialized vocabulary. You might want to post a list of the important words to help students get started.

Note: *The following illustrates the booklet described in Quick Hints.*

Solar system	Comets
Sun, planets	Oval-shaped, gaseous
Spinning, revolving, moving	Orbiting, streaking, blazing
Nine planets are whirling around the sun.	A large tail of dust and ice is blazing around the sun.
...e	Body
...us	Eclipse
...ting, freezing	Dark, mysterious
...this body.	Creeping, gobbling, casting
	Total darkness covers the moon.
	Shadow

Writing to maintain consistent person

EXPLANATION: Students need to learn that a story or composition may be written from three points of view: first, second, or third person. They must also learn to establish a consistent point of view within a piece of writing, a challenging task for many young writers.

Skill Focus

Writing to maintain consistent person

Materials & Resources

☆ Books written in first or third person (suggested book: *My Rotten Redheaded Older Brother* by Patricia Polacco)

Quick Hints

After reading a favorite book with the class, have students respond to it in two pieces of writing. Each piece should use a different person (viewpoint). First, tell them to write a letter to the author telling him or her what they thought of the book. This piece will be written in first person. Then have them write a paragraph *about* the author, based on research they have done. This piece will be written in third person. (Ultimately, these short author biographies might be compiled into a class book called "Our Favorite Authors.")

STEPS

1. Start by explaining to students that the English language includes three possible persons, or points of view, for writing. We can write in the first person, the second person, or the third person. On a transparency or handout, provide a list of first-, second-, and third-person pronouns.

   First-person pronouns: *I, me, my, mine, we, our, ours*

   Second-person pronouns: *you, your, yours*

   Third-person pronouns: *he, she, it, they, him, her, hers, its, them their, theirs*

   As you discuss the list with students, explain that most stories and articles are written in either the first or third person. They will learn how to write in the second person (i.e., "You are nice"; "You need to come here") at another time.

2. Tell students that they need to be careful to choose one person and stay with it during a piece of writing. Writers need to maintain a point of view so that readers can understand and follow along easily.

3. Introduce *My Rotten Redheaded Older Brother* by Patricia Polacco. Read the book aloud, stopping after several sentences in the opening paragraph to ask students to help you identify which person is used (first person). After you have finished reading the whole story, go back through the book and call on volunteers to identify the first-person pronouns throughout.

4. Finally, using a transparency, write several sentences in which the person shifts. Have students help you to underline the pronouns that indicate person and then to identify the problem in each sentence. (In each example, the first pronoun is the correct one; the other pronouns in the example should be changed to match the first.) Below are three sample sentences:

   (me)

   <u>I</u> was a brave little girl, but there were three things that scared <u>her</u>.

   (Her)   (she)

   Her hair was short and brown. <u>My</u> friends thought <u>I</u> looked

   (she)

   very pretty right after <u>I</u> washed her hair.

   (My)

   <u>I</u> sang in the chorus at school. <u>His</u> voice was as smooth as velvet.

Varying sentence structure

EXPLANATION: Learning how to change simple sentences into complex ones improves a student's quality of writing. It is one of the few skills that has a positive impact on writing even when it is practiced in isolation. (Hillocks, 1987)

Skill Focus

Varying sentence structure; using literary models to develop and refine writing

Materials & Resources

☆ Books that demonstrate varied sentence structure and beautiful language (used in this lesson: *My Great-Aunt Arizona* by Gloria Houston)

Quick Hints

As a follow-up, return to one of your previous pieces of writing and model this lesson's concept by combining several of your original, shorter sentences. Show students how writers can make use of ordinary coordinating conjunctions (*and, or, but, yet*) to combine closely related points into one longer, more interesting sentence. Invite students to return to some of their own earlier writing and to revise it by using this technique.

STEPS

1. During the mini-lesson, or as part of your regular read aloud time, read *My Great-Aunt Arizona* to the class. You might introduce it by saying something like, "Boys and girls, this is one of my favorite stories because it's about a woman who taught for 57 years."

2. After reading the story, remark how well it flows and how beautiful the language is. Point out that there are only two sentences on the first double-page spread. Tell students, "There may be only two sentences, but they are very strong sentences with many details. I really like the way the author combined so many details into one sentence."

3. Now write the first sentence on a transparency. Use the book's own "poetic prose" format:

   My great-aunt Arizona
   was born in a log cabin
   her papa built
   in the meadow
   on Henson Creek
   in the Blue Ridge Mountains.

4. Follow up by challenging students, "Let's see just how many thoughts the author combined into this sentence." Write the following, encouraging students to help you as you extract all the facts from this one poetic sentence.

   I have a great-aunt named Arizona.
   She was born in a log cabin.
   Her papa built the log cabin.
   It was built in a meadow.
   The meadow is on Henson Creek.
   The creek is in the Blue Ridge Mountains.

5. Ask one student (one of your better readers) to read back through Gloria Houston's sentence. Then have six different students read aloud the six short sentences you've written. Guide the students to see the difference in the flow. Conclude by saying something like, "Wow! She took six details that could have made six sentences and combined them into one magnificent sentence! I think we should all think about that when we're writing. I think that short, choppy sentences sometimes distract us from the beauty of the language, don't you?" (Hopefully, your instruction and enthusiasm will mean they agree!)

Creating voice in writing

EXPLANATION: Young writers typically use exclamation marks or underlining to show voice. This mini-lesson will help your students establish voice in their writing in more sophisticated ways—through vivid and precise vocabulary.

Skill Focus

Using voice

Materials & Resources

☆ Books that demonstrate strong voice, including these recommended books:

Junie B. Jones and Some Sneaky Peeky Spying by Barbara Park

Stevie by John Steptoe

Owl Moon by Jane Yolen

Scarecrow by Cynthia Rylant

Quick Hints

Cut sticky notes into three to five strips per note (vertically so that each strip is still connected at the top, sticky part). Provide these to students. Have them look back through drafts of their free writing assignments. They should check their own writing to locate examples of voice. Explain that when they find an example, they should tear off a sticky strip and use it to mark the example. Encourage students to share their examples orally.

STEPS

1. Tell students that today you will be reading aloud excerpts from a book that has a strong and interesting author voice. Explain that this means that an author uses vivid and precise vocabulary to assist his or her readers in visualizing the characters and their thoughts and actions.

2. Read an excerpt from your selected book. (*Junie B. Jones and Some Sneaky Peeky Spying* by Barbara Park works well for this lesson.) As you read, ask students to pay particular attention to the author's techniques—especially her use of first-person conversation and lively and carefully chosen vocabulary. Her words and her style seem to lift her voice right off the page, almost as if she were talking right to her audience. Below is one excerpt (from page 2) that exemplifies voice:

   "Spying is when you be very quiet… I am a very good spier. That's because I have sneaky feet. And my nose doesn't whistle when I breathe."

3. Explain to students that sometimes writers can choose better, more interesting words if they actually hear the words out loud before they write them down. (We call this "floating words in the air.") Model this process for students. Refer to the excerpt above and substitute other interesting words that Junie B. Jones could use to show that she is a good spier. Tell the class to listen as you orally experiment with language that focuses on voice. Below is one rephrased version of the excerpt:

   "Spying is when you are sneaky. I am good at being sneaky. I can slip by the teacher with lightning-fast speed. I can hide in a space the size of a mouse hole."

4. Give students an opportunity to think of other ways Junie B. Jones could tell how she is good at spying in kindergarten. Encourage them to first "float the words on air" and then to write down two to four sentences to demonstrate voice.

Using several sources

Skill Focus

Using several sources for a piece of writing

Materials & Resources

☆ Two books that deal with a similar topic in different ways (books used in this lesson: *Dr. White* by Jane Goodall *Animals as Friends* by Sally Morgan)

Quick Hints

Use graphic organizers to help students compare and contrast information from multiple sources. Below are three possible formats (each number refers to a source):

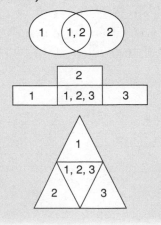

STEPS

1. Read aloud to the class two different selections that address the same topic in different ways. Of the two books we have chosen for this lesson, one—*Dr. White*—is a story based on true events and the other—*Animals as Friends*—is an informational book.

2. Explain the purpose of the lesson by saying something like, "Today I want to show you how we might write about what we've learned from different books or sources. I'm going to write about two books we've read that have related ideas and subject matter."

3. Ask students, "Who remembers the main character in *Dr. White*?" Review that Dr. White was a dog who offered therapy to sick children in a hospital. Discuss the story with the class, inviting students to add details about this dog and what he did to help the children.

4. Continue by saying something like, "You might have wondered if that could really happen. Could dogs really help people get well? Well, remember that we next read an informational book, *Animals as Friends*. That's when we were told again that animals *can* help people in many ways. I'm going to make some notes from the book."

5. Using a transparency, model for students how you find information in this book. Thumb through it and make a written list, including statements such as:

   Touching animals and watching animals can help people relax.

   Tests show that animals can improve people's health.

   Some doctors put fish in their waiting rooms to calm people.

   Taking care of animals helps people exercise.

5. Tell your students that you're going to put together what you've learned from both books and combine it into one paragraph. Below is a sample paragraph:

Animals as Doctors

We read about Dr. White, a little dog, who helped to heal sick children in a hospital. The dog comforted children and took their minds off their illnesses. This was based on a true story, but we all wondered how much of it was true. Could this really happen? Then we read *Animals as Friends*. It told us that animals really can help people feel better. Animals have even saved people's lives. Some doctors and hospitals really do use animals to help sick people. Animals are really helpful to people.

Conclude by adding something like, "I'm glad that I read both of those books that helped me learn more about animals!"

Writing for Real Purposes and Audiences

S tudents are motivated to revise and edit their writing when they know that there is a real purpose and audience for it. Yes, they want to please the teacher, but when they know that others—especially their peers— will read what they've written, they really become interested in doing their best. Ralph Fletcher (1993) said it so well: "You don't learn to write by going through a series of preset exercises. You learn to write by grappling with a real subject that truly matters to you."

So, what truly matters to second and third graders? Here is just a sampling of what we've found in our many years of experience. For these grades, real purposes might involve:

☆ Writing letters to favorite authors and hoping to get a response.

☆ While studying health topics, writing to medical and government sources to receive pamphlets for class reading bins.

☆ Composing original stories based on rich examples read and discussed in the classroom, and then publishing these stories for all to read.

☆ Generating notes with get-well wishes for sick students.

☆ E-mailing pen pals in other states.

☆ Producing a class newsletter to be shared with other classes at the same grade level.

These are just a few examples. The list of purposes and audiences that motivate students to write is inexhaustible!

There is another important reason to provide real purposes and audiences for students who are learning to write. Indeed, perhaps the greatest lesson of all that we can give students is to help them discover that there is power in writing. They need to understand firsthand that writing can get results— even if you're only eight or nine years old. Even young students can discover that writing evokes emotions of all kinds—laughter, fear, tears, and joy. It can stimulate discussions and generate new ideas. Writing brings results—e-mails from friends, pamphlets from faraway places, samples of products. It carries the power to persuade and to help us form decisions that can affect our whole lives. Writing can open all of these portals to the world and so many more, and students in primary grades are ready and able to experience the riches that writing can provide. It's our job as teachers to give them these opportunities.

Let's take a look now at a number of lessons that will motivate your students as they discover the power of writing.

Students in this class record their observations in learning logs.

This class is integrating technology into their writing.

> Harris
> Don't worry! The teachers are nice. When you do somthing good.in reading or Math in Mrs Culler's room

> she will give you skittles

This is a note written by a second grader in his first week of school to a first grader to allay the "first-grade jitters."

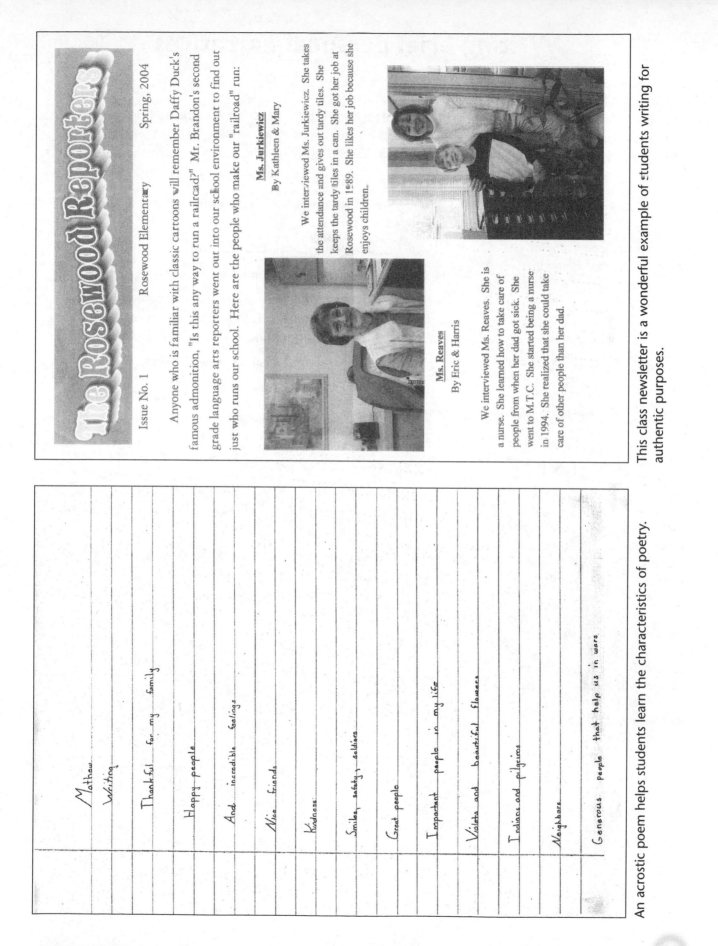

The Rosewood Reporters

Issue No. 1   Rosewood Elementary   Spring, 2004

Anyone who is familiar with classic cartoons will remember Daffy Duck's famous admonition, "Is this any way to run a railroad?" Mr. Brandon's second grade language arts reporters went out into our school environment to find out just who runs our school. Here are the people who make our "railroad" run:

Ms. Jurkiewicz
By Kathleen & Mary

We interviewed Ms. Jurkiewicz. She takes the attendance and gives out tardy tiles. She keeps the tardy tiles in a can. She got her job at Rosewood in 1989. She likes her job because she enjoys children.

Ms. Reaves
By Eric & Harris

We interviewed Ms. Reaves. She is a nurse. She learned how to take care of people from when her dad got sick. She went to M.T.C. She started being a nurse in 1994. She realized that she could take care of other people than her dad.

This class newsletter is a wonderful example of students writing for authentic purposes.

Mathew

Writing

Thankful for my family

Happy people

And incredible feelings

Nice friends

Kindness

Smiles, safety, soldiers

Great people

Important people in my life

Violets and beautiful flowers

Indians and pilgrims

Neighbors

Generous people that help us in wars

An acrostic poem helps students learn the characteristics of poetry.

Writing brief personal narratives

EXPLANATION: Many students choose to write personal narratives during their free writing time. Young writers, who have had minimal exposure to literature and other kinds of writing, quite naturally find it easier to write from their personal point of view about something that really happened.

STEPS

1. Tell students that this lesson focuses on writing brief personal stories. Explain that, even when writing personal narratives like these, writers must follow specific criteria. For instance, they must:

   ☆ Use first-person pronouns.

   ☆ Choose interesting words that stimulate the senses of the audience.

   ☆ Include a beginning, middle, and end.

   ☆ Show an awareness of audience and purpose.

2. Using a transparency, model writing a one-paragraph personal narrative. A sample paragraph follows. As you write, think aloud about how you are incorporating the four criteria listed above.

My First Lesson in Water Skiing

Splash! "Try again." Splash! "Try again." These were the encouraging words from my Uncle Bobby, who taught me to water ski. Even though my arms were tired and my legs were shaking, I was determined to learn this sport. It took all of a hot summer afternoon to stay up on the skis for longer than three minutes! After many falls, I finally skied behind the boat and then crossed the wake onto smooth water. It felt so good as everyone in the ski boat clapped and cheered. Then it was my turn to ride in the boat and cheer on another skier!

3. Invite students to write their own one-paragraph personal narratives. As they write, circulate around the room, checking to make sure that they are incorporating the specific criteria and helping them as needed.

Note: The following illustrates the timeline described in Quick Hints.

+	rode a tricycle	learned to skate		started school			brother born
Age	3	4	5	6	7	8	
–	broke my arm	moved away					

Skill Focus

Writing brief personal narratives

Materials & Resources

☆ A transparency of a one-paragraph personal narrative

Quick Hints

Invite those students who write entries in personal journals or diaries to select one entry and to develop it into a personal narrative. Additionally, you might ask them to make a timeline of their lives. Tell them to put a + above the line to indicate a good experience or a – below the line to mark a bad experience. (See the end of this lesson for an illustration of a timeline.)

Writing in response

Preliminary Considerations:

Within a book or story that students are about to read, select excerpts in the text that you believe are important for students to think about and process. (Storm in the Night by Mary Stolz works well for this lesson.) On the left side of a double-entry response journal, write down the key words and phrases and page numbers of these excerpts. Create a transparency from this material.

STEPS

1. Explain to students that a double-entry response journal has two columns. The left-hand column contains the text or material that will need a response; the right-hand column is blank and is to be filled in by the journal writer. There are many kinds of double-entry response journals (see Quick Hints for an additional alternative), but they all follow this pattern.

2. Begin by saying something like, "Today we're going to use a double-entry response journal to help us think about what we're reading. First, I'll show you what I would write in a double-entry journal, and then I'll give you a chance to write in one, too. Once you learn how to do this, we'll be using these journals often in our class."

3. Using the transparency, point out, "Boys and girls, you can see that there is already some writing in the left-hand column of my response journal. The page numbers written here will remind me to stop on that page. The print will tell me to stop and think. Sometimes it'll be a question I need to answer or sometimes it'll be a few words from the page that I just need to share my thoughts about. Let me show you how."

4. Read the story aloud until you reach the page numbers and specific lines you have highlighted on the response form. Then stop for a moment, think aloud, and write a response in the right-hand column. A sample based on Stolz's *Storm in the Night* follows:

Double-Entry Response Journal

When it comes to this...	here's what I think
Pg. 110 "A grandfather could be a boy, if he went back in his memory far enough; but a boy could not be a grandfather."	I think the boy is saying his grandfather can easily be a boy because he has the memories. But the boy doesn't have memories of being old yet.
Pg. 174 "I can hear better in the dark than I can when the lights are on."	I guess we all pay close attention when we're not distracted by other senses. I understand that.

Skill Focus

Writing in response to something one has read

Materials & Resources

☆ A transparency based on the format in Step 4, with left-hand column filled in before the lesson

☆ Short story or book (recommended book: *Storm in the Night* by Mary Stolz

Quick Hints

Double-entry response journals can also be used for students to reread and respond to their own writing. This teaches students to evaluate their own work. After reading through a student's paper, include personalized prompts in the left-hand column, thereby making students stop and reflect at these spots. For instance, you might fill in: "Paragraph 2—importance of this character to the story" and the student would respond to this prompt in the right-hand column.

Three-Part Lesson: Writing a Friendly Letter

Part 1: **Planning**

> **EXPLANATION:** Students usually enjoy writing friendly letters, because they like writing for a real purpose and audience. It is also fulfilling for them to realize that their writing can yield results—for instance, a response from the person they addressed.

Preliminary Considerations:

Before beginning this lesson, we recommend that you allow students to design their own personal stationery for friendly letters. You might provide a standard word-processing template to which students can add their own stationery designs in the borders. Let each student make one or two designs. Photocopy a small supply of stationery of each student's design and store it in a snap-seal bag. They'll be proud to have produced their own personalized stationery! Don't forget to design your own stationery as well.

STEPS

1. Using a transparency of your template for modeling, start the lesson by explaining that letters follow a specific format. Point to each of the elements of the letter highlighted below as you discuss it with students. (Aspects you'll discuss are detailed in Steps 2 through 6 below.)

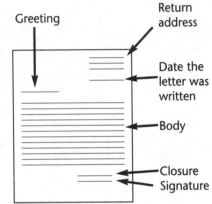

2. Explain that the return address must include capital letters for streets, cities, and states. (Postal initials of states are now widely used.) Zip codes must also be included here.

3. Let students know that most informal, friendly letters start with a greeting of "Dear," followed by the person's name. (Tell them that they should use the form of the name that they commonly use when they speak to or about the person.) The name must be capitalized since it's a proper noun, and a comma should follow the name.

4. Stress that friendly letters need to provide specific details as well as show interest in the person addressed.

5. Give students a choice of closures for friendly letters. Point out that the first word is capitalized, the second is not, and a comma always concludes the closure. Here are a few closures that you might suggest:

   Yours truly,   Sincerely,   Your friend,   Best wishes,

6. Finally, using the same template transparency, start at the top of the stationery and fill in all spots with your own personal information (or that of a fictional person). For the body of the letter, write a few interesting sentences that both describe yourself and inquire about the addressee. Tell students that they will have a chance to work with this letter again in a subsequent lesson.

Skill Focus

Writing friendly letters; capitalizing proper nouns and titles; using capital letters in greetings and closings of letters (planning)

Materials & Resources

☆ Stationery template

☆ A transparency of your own personalized stationery template

☆ Large snap-seal bags (1/2 gal. size) or 9- by 11-inch envelopes (one per student) for storage of personalized stationery

Quick Hints

Students might enjoy the opportunity to trade some of the stationery they've designed with their classmates. Have students put six of their sheets of stationery on a cabinet. Line up the piles of stationery so that all of the designs can be seen. First, let students walk by to see all of the clever creations. Then allow them to "shop" for six new designs they would like to add to their own collection of stationery.

Three-Part Lesson: Writing a Friendly Letter

Part 2: Learning what makes a good friendly letter

EXPLANATION: Letter writing is an art as well as a skill. It takes a great deal of thought to allow your genuine voice to come through in a letter and at the same time to show concern for the person you're addressing. Today's lesson stresses those points.

Skill Focus

Writing friendly letters; capitalizing proper nouns and titles; using capital letters in greetings and closings of letters

Materials & Resources

☆ Letter puzzles (either precut or as whole pages); one set per group of students (see Appendices, pages 119–120)

☆ 10 pieces of unlined paper

☆ One pair of scissors per group

Quick Hints

Postcards can also enable students to practice writing correct addresses and include colorful details. Because postcards provide such a small amount of space, the task can be quite challenging. This is an opportunity for students to learn that one colorful detail is better than several general sentences. You might create a postcard template (four postcards to one sheet of paper) on your computer and copy it onto card-stock paper. Invite students to illustrate their own cards.

STEPS

1. Review the parts of the friendly letter presented in Part 1 of this lesson. With help from volunteers, name the parts, the purposes they serve, and their proper position on the stationery.

2. Tell students that they are going to put some letter puzzles together to show that they understand where things go in a letter. They will also judge these letters to see which one is the most interesting to read.

3. Divide the class into small cooperative groups. Give each group two sheets of unlined paper and the two pages of letter puzzles (see Appendix, pages 119–120). If you have not precut the pieces, have the groups do this.

4. Ask students to assemble the two letters, each on one sheet of paper, paying attention to where the parts need to go and where punctuation marks should be placed. Circulate among the groups as they complete this task.

5. Ask students to discuss within their groups which letter they think is better written and why they've reached that conclusion. Tell them to be prepared to share the results of their discussion with the class.

6. Students should conclude that Letter #1 is the better letter because it includes specific details and shows interest in the reader. That's the kind of letter we want to write—and that we look forward to receiving!

7. Conclude this lesson by sharing with students some of the many different reasons writers may have for writing friendly letters. For instance, they may wish to stay in touch with someone who has moved away; to thank someone for a gift; or to discover new things about others who live in different regions.

Three-Part Lesson: Writing a Friendly Letter

Part 3: Using correct punctuation for letters and envelopes

EXPLANATION: As students learn about letter writing, they also learn to use the correct conventions that accompany it. This lesson exposes them to many rules of capitalization beyond the one they're already most familiar with (use a capital letter to start a sentence).

Skill Focus

Writing a friendly letter (addressing the envelope); using capital letters for proper nouns (cities, states, titles, months, names); using correct punctuation with cities, states, dates

Materials & Resources

☆ Transparency of your friendly letter from Part 1 (page 84)

☆ Student-made envelopes or purchased envelopes (inexpensive if purchased in bulk)

☆ Colored transparency markers

Quick Hints

You may find that it is useful to provide a list of state postal abbreviations (which you can find at www.usps.com) as a resource in your classroom. They can be posted in your Writing Center for students' use, provided to students as a handout to keep in their writing folders, or included in a directory in your reference area.

STEPS

1. Display the transparency of the letter you've written to your friend (from Part 1 of this lesson). Ask volunteers to come forward to underline one capitalized word apiece. Have them explain why they think that word needs to be capitalized.

2. Make a checklist on the chalkboard of the types of words that require capitalization; place a check in the column each time one of those types is represented and identified in your letter. A sample checklist is at right.

In letters, we capitalize:	
Names of people (including our signatures)	√ √
Names of cities	√
Names of states	√
Words that start sentences	√ √ √ √
Greetings	√
First words of closures	√
Months of the year	√

3. Highlight on your chart the two items that are specific to letter writing. Stress that the others are used in all types of writing—we always capitalize those, including within letters.

4. Tell students that you want their advice about completing the envelope to mail your letter. On the transparency, sketch the shape of an envelope. Allow students to refer to the chart you've completed to help you as you fill out the envelope. A completed example follows:

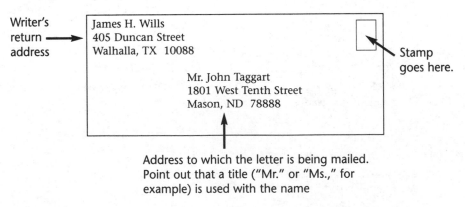

Writer's return address → James H. Wills / 405 Duncan Street / Walhalla, TX 10088

Stamp goes here.

Mr. John Taggart / 1801 West Tenth Street / Mason, ND 78888

Address to which the letter is being mailed. Point out that a title ("Mr." or "Ms.," for example) is used with the name

5. Distribute envelopes to students. Ask each student to address an envelope to a friend or family member, using correct form.

Two-Part Lesson: Writing a Persuasive Letter

Part 1: **Planning**

EXPLANATION: Young students often express strong feelings, such as, "That book was terrible!" At the same time they must learn to support their opinions with equally strong reasons. This is the only way that a piece of writing can be genuinely persuasive. Planning is key to crafting a persuasive letter, and that phase is the focus of this lesson.

Skill Focus

Writing a persuasive letter (planning)

Materials & Resources

☆ Transparency made from persuasive letter organizational template (see Appendix, page 121)

Quick Hints

Group students in pairs and have each pair brainstorm topics about sports, video games, movies, and so on. Have partners choose one of four different purposes—to entertain, to explain, to persuade, or to describe—in order to write a brief composition about the brainstormed topic. After writing, ask each student in the pair to figure out his or her partner's purpose for writing.

STEPS

1. Inform students that we celebrate Earth Day on April 22. Provide facts about why the day was established. (In 1970 as people grew more aware of the effects of pollution, Earth Day was created. As our cities were covered by dense clouds of smoke and some animals were endangered, our government created the Environmental Protection Act, or E.P.A.) Describe for students some of the ways in which people observe this day (recycling glass, metal, paper, and plastic; planting trees; walking instead of riding in a car; turning off lights when not in use, etc.). Build interest in the fact that the school does not observe this day and has no plan for recycling, and so on; stress, too, that such activities would be very helpful to the environment.

   Note: If your school does celebrate Earth Day, make this a fictitious situation. You might make it more compelling for students by tying that situation to a real-life experience—for instance, the school that you or a good friend attended.

2. Tell students that one step they might take in a situation like this is to write a persuasive letter to the principal of the school. This kind of letter follows a special format—it needs to include both a clear statement of the writer's point of view and a set of supportive reasons.

3. Using a transparency of the persuasive letter template (see below and Appendix, page 121), model how to structure a letter to the principal proposing ways the school should celebrate Earth Day. As you fill in this organizational plan, point out all the important elements that need to be included in a persuasive letter. Tell students that in the next lesson, the class will write the actual letter based on this plan. A sample filled-in template follows:

Focus on the audience of the writing. Mr. Warren, the principal
State your opinion, idea, or point of view. We believe our school should participate in Earth Day.
Write support for your opinion. (Include at least 3 reasons.) 1. Paper is wasted. 2. Plastic utensils are thrown away. 3. There are no trees on the school grounds.
Restate your opinion. We should do our part in protecting the environment.

Two-Part Lesson: Writing a Persuasive Letter

Part 2: **Using the organizational plan**

EXPLANATION: Young students often express strong feelings, such as, "That book was terrible!" At the same time they must learn to support their opinions with equally strong reasons. This is the only way that a piece of writing can be genuinely persuasive. In this lesson, the class gets to actually write the letter that has been previously outlined.

Skill Focus

Writing a persuasive letter

Materials & Resources

☆ Photocopies, one for each student, of the organizational planning template (Appendix, page 121)

Quick Hints

Have students tape record their own letters for others to enjoy. You may discover an additional benefit in this process: Often, as students read their own work orally, they identify spots that need further editing or revision.

STEPS

1. Review the organizational plan template that you created with the class in the previous lesson. Have volunteers read the points aloud.

2. Using a new transparency, model writing a persuasive letter based on the points identified. As you write, stop to think aloud about how and why you are incorporating the points and weaving them into paragraphs that build the letter. Below is a sample letter based on the organizational plan from Part 1 of this lesson:

> February 5, 2005
>
> Dear Mr. Warren,
>
> In April 1970, to protect our environment, a Wisconsin senator established Earth Day. Our class recently observed ways that our school trashes instead of protects the environment. Every day many sheets of paper are thrown away. In our class, we counted in one day that almost 100 pieces went into the trashcan. In the cafeteria, plastic forks and spoons are purchased, used, and thrown away. These plastic utensils end up in a landfill that harms our earth. When we look outside our classroom window, there are no trees in sight. Cutting down trees and not replacing them is bad for our environment.
>
> Our class believes that there are many ways our school should participate in this important event. We would like to suggest that we write or copy on both sides of the paper and then participate in the city's paper-recycling program. This would save trees! Next, we think that using metal utensils that can be washed and reused is a smart way to cut down on waste for landfills. Also, we believe that planting trees would beautify our school grounds and keep our air clean. By acting on some or all of these things, we will be doing our part to protect the environment.
>
> Thank you for reading our letter. We hope you will agree with us and will let us help plan our first Earth Day!
>
> Sincerely,
>
> Miss Johnson's Third-Grade Class

3. Finally, discuss additional issues that might motivate someone to write a persuasive letter. Distribute photocopies of the organizational template and help students to fill in the forms and then to write their own persuasive letters based on their plans.

Two-Part Lesson: Writing a News Article
Part 1: **Planning**

> **EXPLANATION:** This lesson introduces students to the journalistic style used in news articles. Often referred to as "5W writing," news articles must address these five basics: who, what, why, when, and where. Typically, answering these 5 Ws should occur within the first paragraph or sentence.

Skill Focus

Writing a news article (planning)

Materials & Resources

☆ Sample news article

☆ Cards from Appendix, pages 122–123 (you can cut out these cards before the lesson, or have student groups cut them out during the lesson)

Quick Hints

As follow-up, collect news articles that you feel will be appealing to students. In our experience, three basic types of reading materials always prove popular: those that tickle the funny bone, touch the heart, or gross students out! You can be certain that almost any newspaper contains examples of all three on a daily basis. Have students read through articles you select and highlight answers to the 5 Ws, each in a different color. You might wish to laminate the articles beforehand so that they can be used repeatedly.

STEPS

1. On the chalkboard, write:

   Who?   What?   Why?   When?   Where?

2. Tell students that news articles are arranged in a special way. The most important facts are reported immediately in the first sentence or paragraph, and usually that information includes the answers to the questions who, what, why, when, and where.

3. Place students in five groups. Explain that you want the class to be detectives during this lesson. Distribute to each group five cards with the answers to the questions listed on the chalkboard (see Appendix, pages 122–123). They should discuss the information on the five cards and be prepared to match the correct information with its corresponding question.

4. After adequate time, ask each group of detectives to come to the chalkboard and tape each answer underneath the appropriate question. Have students read the information aloud to the rest of the class. If done correctly, each group's taped answers should form a complete, informative sentence.

5. Make a transparency of a news article (one of your choosing that your students will enjoy). Ask students to listen carefully as you read the article for their enjoyment.

6. Ask the small groups to work together again to identify the 5 Ws in this article. Have each group share their findings aloud, or invite them to come to the chalkboard and write an answer to one of the Ws that they have identified.

Two-Part Lesson: Writing a News Article

Part 2: **Writing the news article**

EXPLANATION: Now that students have learned about the organizational pattern of a news article, this lesson lets them have fun plugging relevant information into the pattern. And this news article has a twist!

Skill Focus

Writing a news article

Materials & Resources

☆ A selection of books of folk and fairy tales and nursery rhymes

Quick Hints

You might compile the articles students write during this lesson into a newspaper that the children can take home to share with their parents. There are many good computer programs available that can provide a newspaper format for you. Think about having the class write news articles using social studies, science, or health content: "Nation Elects First President," "Pilgrims Share Thanksgiving with Native Indians," "New Planet Discovered," etc.

STEPS

1. Quickly review the previous day's lesson by asking students to recall the five important pieces of information that journalists always try to include in the first paragraph of a news article. As students share them, write the words, followed by question marks, on the chalkboard.

2. Announce to the class, "Boys and girls, I've got some shocking news to share with you! You're not going to believe what happened! I'm going to write the news just as a reporter would. First I'll organize the important details by listing the 5Ws." Then write the following on the chalkboard:

   Who?   Red Riding Hood and Grandmother
   What?   Were attacked by a wolf
   Why?   Red Riding Hood talked to a stranger in the woods
   When?   Yesterday afternoon
   Where?   At her grandmother's house in the woods

3. On a transparency, model for students how to use this information to write a good first paragraph for your article. Remember to tell students that paragraphs for news article are generally short and to the point. Below is one possible sample.

   ### Wolf Attacks Girl and Grandmother
   Yesterday afternoon, Red Riding Hood, of 34 Wolf Lane, was attacked by a wolf that surprised her as she delivered cookies to her grandmother who lives at 613 Deep Woods Lane. A witness reported that young Hood stopped to talk to the dangerous wolf in the forest and told him where she was heading. The sly wolf was then able to surprise both victims.

4. Invite students to thumb through the books of folk and fairy tales and nursery rhymes and to try writing their own news articles based on these stories. Possible headlines include: "Owner of Glass Slipper Found After Long Search" (*Cinderella*); "Wolf Destroys Homes" (*Three Little Pigs*); "Girl Falls Ill After Choking on Apple" (*Snow White*); "Boy Missing" (*Jack and Beanstalk*); and "Woman Found Living in Shoe with Children" (*The Old Woman Who Lived in a Shoe*).

5. When all of the articles are complete, you might collect them and bind them into a class edition of "Fairyland News."

Writing a cinquain (unrhymed) poem

EXPLANATION: The fact that writing that is unrhymed can still be defined as poetry may come as quite a shock to second and third graders. Students who haven't developed a preference for this genre may find the unrhymed poetry appealing because of its short, concise, descriptive language.

Skill Focus

Writing poems that are unrhymed

Materials & Resources

☆ Transparency or display chart with rules for writing a cinquain poem

☆ Pre-selected topic (preferably from the class's literature or content area books)

☆ Word list you've culled from that book

Quick Hints

Use cinquain poems as a way to get students to respond to literature. After reading a selection, ask students to write a cinquain that describes the main character, the setting, or the problem in the story. This type of poetry can also be used to elicit responses to concepts learned in content studies.

STEPS

1. Tell students that they're going to encounter a new kind of poetry. In this kind of poetry, none of the lines rhyme. And this particular kind of poem, called a *cinquain* poem, has to follow a special format: It always has five lines, and each line does something special. Using your transparency or chart, display the following rules for the class. Discuss each direction as you go down the list.

How to Write a Cinquain Poem

1. **First line:** Write one word that tells the subject of the poem.
2. **Second line:** Write two words that describe the subject and separate them with a comma.
3. **Third line:** Write three action words ending in "-ing" that tell what the subject does and put commas between them.
4. **Fourth line:** Tell in one short sentence how the subject of the poem makes you feel and end the line with a period.
5. **Fifth line:** Write another word that is a synonym for the subject.

2. On a transparency, present to the class the list of words you've jotted down about the pre-selected topic. For example, for a poem on a lunar eclipse, your list might look like this:

Words that relate to lunar eclipses

casts	falls	covering	turns dark
shadows	moon	slowly	total

3. Following the directions that you've displayed, write a cinquain poem on a transparency. Below is a sample cinquain based on the above word list.

> Eclipse
> Dark, mysterious
> Creeping, gobbling, casting
> Total darkness covers the moon.
> Shadow

4. Either as a separate follow-up or at the end of this lesson, invite students to write their own cinquain poems. Be sure they start by choosing a topic and creating a word list based on that topic. The directions in Step 1 should remain posted while students compose their poems, so that they can follow them carefully. You may want to photocopy the directions so that they can become a permanent part of students' writing folders.

Learning about rhymed and unrhymed poems

EXPLANATION: By second and third grade students begin to understand the characteristics that make poetry a genre of its own. This lesson helps students arrive at a deeper understanding of the nature of poetry.

Skill Focus

Writing poems that are unrhymed

Materials & Resources

☆ Cinquain poem from previous lesson

☆ A rhyming poem on same subject

☆ Blank Venn diagram

Quick Hints

Expose students to a variety of poetry. Keep your classroom library stocked with anthologies and collections. Display individual poems around the room. Poetry makes a great introduction to content topics, a wonderful read-aloud, and enjoyable independent reading for students.

Use the opportunity that poetry offers to underscore for students that not all writing follows conventions. For example, the cinquain—as with a good deal of other poetry—doesn't use complete sentences or standard end punctuation. Poetry has its own characteristics, and poets "break rules" all the time.

STEPS

1. On a transparency or chart paper, display the cinquain poem from the previous lesson next to a poem that rhymes. (See below for the cinquain and for a sample rhyming poem.) Read both poems aloud. Divide the class and ask one half to practice reading the cinquain for a few minutes and the other half to practice reading the rhyming verse. Have them continue until they feel that they are reading with total fluency.

Lunar Eclipse
Spinning forces start their race
As shadows creep across its face
There is no need to cause us fear
Soon a bright, round moon
    will reappear.

Eclipse
Dark, mysterious
Creeping, gobbling, casting
Total darkness covers the moon.
Shadow

2. Invite each group to recite its poem chorally, using excellent poetic voices, for the class. Students will see that poems are fun to share aloud and sometimes more enjoyable if they're heard.

3. Lead the class in a discussion about how the pieces are alike and how they are different. One effective way to do this is to have the students help you fill in a Venn diagram on a transparency or on the chalkboard. A sample diagram is below:

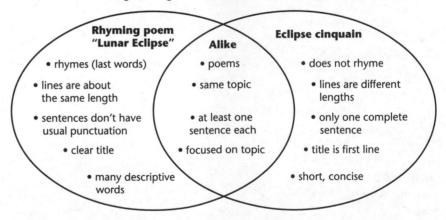

4. After analyzing how these poems are alike and different, review with students what all poetry has in common. You might start a chart like that below; students can add points to it as they continue to explore poetry during the school year.

   Poetry...
   √ Doesn't use standard rules of grammar.
   √ Creates a picture for the reader.
   √ Uses few, well-chosen words to say a great deal.

Two-Part Lesson: Writing and Presenting a Book Report

Part 1: **Writing a summary**

EXPLANATION: Book reports should be interesting, not dull; lively, not boring; organized, not chaotic. This lesson provides a matrix of interesting formats for both written and oral presentations, from which students can select the kind of book report they'd like to do. The focus here is on written assignments.

Skill Focus

Writing and presenting a book report (written format)

Materials & Resources

☆ Photocopies of the BOOK-O Book Report Matrix form (see Appendix, page 124)

☆ Age-appropriate book (used in this lesson: *Stage Fright on a Summer Night* by Mary Pope Osborne, #25 in the Magic Tree House series)

Quick Hints

Create a display area for favorite books that students have read. After students have created their written reports, bind these pages and keep them near the books. You may notice that certain books suddenly become very popular—peers have a terrific influence on the books read in your classroom!

STEPS

1. Distribute to each student a photocopy of the BOOK-O Book Report Matrix (see Appendix, page 124). Tell the class that this sheet may look a lot like a Bingo card, but it's really all about the many interesting ways to do book reports. Discuss each box with students and explain that some choices are better suited to written assignments, some to oral presentations, and some can be used for both.

2. Explain that you will model the process of selecting a format, then writing a book report based on your selection.

3. Tell students that the book you've read for the report is a Magic Tree House book. Because this is a written assignment, your choice for the format you'd like to use is the first box in the matrix: "Write a summary." This might be a summary of the plot, of the characters, or of another aspect of the book. You will demonstrate two kinds of summaries: one summary of the plot and one about the characters.

4. Using a transparency, first model writing a plot summary and then a character summary for this book. During the think aloud, demonstrate for students how to include only the most important facts and details from the book.

Stage Fright on a Summer Night by Mary Pope Osborne

Plot Summary:

Jack and Annie are whisked back in time to Elizabethan England. There they meet William Shakespeare himself, one of the greatest writers of all time. Mr. Shakespeare is having a hard time with some of the actors in his latest show. Jack and Annie act in his play. The Queen of England claps for them. Annie frees a bear headed for a fight and dresses him as an actor. They make a wish in the tree house and return home. What will their next adventure be?

Character Summary:

Jack and Annie are brother and sister. They are eight and seven years old and live in Frog Creek, PA. The two love adventure and in this episode have to turn daytime into night. They travel back in time to England through the magic of the tree house. They learn interesting facts about England along the way. Annie pretends to be a boy so she can be with Jack in Shakespeare's play. They are brilliant in their roles as fairies.

Two-Part Lesson: Writing and Presenting a Book Report
Part 2: Interviewing a character

EXPLANATION: This lesson utilizes the same matrix (presented in Part 1) of book report formats—from which students can select a format they find appealing. The focus here is on oral presentations. Remember that book report assignments may combine both written and oral presentations.

Skill Focus

Writing and presenting a book report (oral presentation)

Materials & Resources

☆ One book (per student) recently read by that student

☆ BOOK-O Book Report Matrix (see Appendix, page 124)

Quick Hints

One way to use the matrix is to invite students to choose a row across, down, or diagonally and to do a three-part book report, comprising the three formats.

We recommend using a rubric to assess the book reports. See Appendix, page 125, for a sample rubric.

Preliminary Considerations:

Before this lesson, students should have read and selected a favorite book about which they'd like to report.

STEPS

1. Call students' attention again to the BOOK-O Book Report Matrix of book report formats from the previous lesson (see Appendix, page 124). Tell them that the class is going to focus on a format that works best for oral presentations: developing a character interview.

2. Have students get out their selected books and take a few moments to review the books. Now tell each student that he or she is to assume the role of one character in the book and to create six to eight interview questions for that character. Below are sample questions:

   Was your character realistic or unrealistic?
   How did your character change?
   What emotions did your character have?
   What did you learn about yourself as the character?
   How did your actions affect the other characters?
   How are you like this character?

3. Invite one student to come to the front of the class. Ask other students to draw the questions and conduct an interview with the character. (As a variation, have students conduct the interviews in pairs, with each student having the chance to be both the character and the interviewer.) Be sure that students understand that they must answer the questions by incorporating details from their character's actions and personality.

Writing in learning logs

STEPS

EXPLANATION: Learning logs allow writers to discover, develop, refine, and define ideas they have studied at their own pace and in their own way. There are no strict guidelines. The important point in keeping a learning log is to write regular entries.

Skill Focus

Writing in learning logs

Materials & Resources

☆ Construction paper

☆ Notebook paper

☆ Colorful ribbon

Quick Hints

How to make a simple learning log: Cut notebook paper in half and staple or bind multiple pages together. Cover with 1/2 sheet of construction paper. Tie up with curly ribbon to present to students. (Also, see directions on page 73 for another handy-size log or notebook.) After you have distributed notebooks to students, encourage them to make creative covers for their own logs.

1. Tell students that you are going to introduce them to a new way of writing. Call their attention to the notebooks you have prepared (see Quick Hints). The notebooks should be ready to present to each student, made to look appealing, perhaps tied in curly ribbon like gifts. Explain that as they study new topics in science, social studies, math, health, and other content areas, you want them to use these new notebooks to write and/or draw about what they are learning.

2. On a transparency, model writing a brief entry based on a topic taught the previous day. Your entry could describe or explain an activity (experiment), an idea, questions generated, or a glossary of important words. The example entry below is based on a science lesson. If you were using this example, you might introduce it by saying something such as, "Remember yesterday in science, we learned about fossils. I think I will make an entry in my learning log about something interesting I learned. I will write what I remember in my own words. I will also write how I connected this information to something I already knew."

   October 22, 2005

   In science class I learned that fossil imprints are molds made in mud or sand. There are more animal fossils than plant fossils. I think this is because plants don't last as long as animals. I know this because in my backyard, a leaf on the ground broke into many pieces almost overnight, but a bird skeleton stayed in one piece for days and days.

3. Finally, present a learning log to each student. Invite them to think about something intriguing or interesting that they learned earlier today or yesterday. Have them enter today's date and, using your model as a guide, write their first entry.

Writing directions

Skill Focus

Writing directions

Materials & Resources

☆ A small surprise for each student in the class (suggestions: stickers, a gold-covered chocolate coin, new writing materials such as journals; or one new gift for the whole class, such as a book they're interested in)

☆ Two versions of a "treasure map" with directions—one on paper and one on a transparency

Quick Hints

After students have polished their skill in writing directions, you might engage them in this fun and genuinely useful class project. Invite them to construct a book of directions to be used by visitors to the school. Assign students locations that can be reached from the main office and have them write step-by-step directions. Be sure to try out the directions first before placing the book in the office!

STEPS

Note: A successful and fun treasure hunt will depend on the right planning ahead on your part. Be sure to take into consideration ahead of time this lesson's unique requirements and the fact that it involves students exploring the school building and perhaps the school grounds. You may need to involve classroom aides and to obtain clearance from the principal. Also, as special preparation for this lesson, you'll need to hide the "treasure" in its designated location and to choose a location that you feel will be just challenging enough, but easily accessible, for students.

1. The treasure map that you prepare ahead for this lesson will need to include, of course, personalized directions for your school. As general guidelines, however, try to:

    ☆ Use imperative sentences (i.e., "Turn left at the office" or "Take 10 steps and stop.")

    ☆ List the directions one step at the time.

    ☆ Use the fewest words possible in each step.

2. Start the lesson by announcing that there is a mystery to solve today. A treasure is "buried" in the school and there's a treasure map for students to use to find it!

3. Using the transparency, present the map with the directions to students. Read aloud the directions before you distribute a copy to each student. Keep a copy for yourself so that you'll have your own set of directions as you follow students on their quest.

4. Have students use their maps to follow the directions to the treasure.

5. After what should be a successful and fun treasure hunt, have students reconvene in the classroom. Hold a class discussion. Focus on the directions students followed to find the treasure. Were they easy or difficult to follow? (Since your directions have been written to provide a good example, students should respond that they were easy to follow.) Review the points you followed in creating clear directions (see Step 1). Emphasize that in imperative sentences the subject that appears to be missing is an understood subject—the reader or "you."

6. Place students in cooperative groups. Tell them it's their chance to show that they can write good directions. Ask them to pretend that there is a new student in your class who needs to get to a specific location in the school. Each group is to write clear directions from the classroom to the location. Give each group a different destination, such as the cafeteria, the office, or the media center.

7. Have each group share its directions with others, either in writing or orally. Help students evaluate the different sets of directions.

You've got mail!

EXPLANATION: Second and third graders enjoy the "instant gratification" that characterizes e-mailing. They can have fun writing with common, acceptable slang, and using cute emoticons (smiley faces). As they engage in what is typically an immediate and informal kind of correspondence, students find it natural to demonstrate voice in their writing.

Skill Focus

Using e-mail to communicate with family and friends

Materials & Resources

☆ Computer with Internet capability, if possible. (In absence of a computer, don't ignore this mode of writing. Just model it, as you do with other writing.)

☆ A prior agreement with a teacher-friend for corresponding via e-mail

Quick Hints

Provide a handout of the following fun emoticons (emotion + icons) that students can use in their e-mails. See if they recognize the punctuation marks that create them:

happy :-)	tired or upset :-/
sad :-(	wink ;-)
surprised :-0	sunglass smile 8-)
baseball fan d:-)	telling secrets :-X

As a follow-up to this lesson, invite students to send you an e-mail from a home computer.

STEPS

1. Discuss with the class two ways available to communicate with friends who aren't close by: letters, postcards, and notes sent through regular mail; or e-mails sent via the Internet. Let them know that there are some real advantages to using e-mail. On the chalkboard or a transparency, list these benefits. See the sample list below:

What I Love About E-mail

I can write quickly without gathering any writing materials.

E-mail doesn't require postage.

The computer can check my spelling.

I can easily send attachments of pictures and other writing.

My computer keeps a copy of what I send and what I receive.

I can send the same e-mail to lots of people at the same time without retyping it.

My e-mail is immediately received by the person I've written to.

I can receive a reply almost immediately! (Our personal favorite reason!)

2. Explain that you're going to write an e-mail to a teacher-friend (get prior permission from your friend) and you'll demonstrate the process as you do it. Bring up your e-mail screen and show students where the address goes. Explain that this address is different from the one that goes on a postal letter and always has these parts:

Special name or nickname the person has chosen → **AAAA@bbbbb.ccc** ← The address, which includes a dot and a suffix, usually "com," "net," or "org"

Symbol (@) that divides the name and the address

3. Warn students that each letter and/or number within the name and address must be typed *exactly* right or the message will end up undeliverable and lost in cyberspace!

4. Show students where your note fits in a special message box on the computer screen. Stress that notes to family and friends can usually be very informal. A sample message follows:

> Hi, David! I just got a new writing mini-lesson book I think you'd like. It's called *Just-Right Writing Lessons.* Are your students writing every day? My students love to write! :-) Hope to hear back! Jill

5. After using "Spell Check" (see lesson on page 26), hit the "Send" button and announce to the class that your message is not only on its way, but already at its destination!

6. When your friend responds (either at that moment, or later in the day), be sure to show students the return message.

Polishing and Publishing Our Writing

Once in a while a piece of writing emerges that stands out from a writer's other compositions, and the writer recognizes (often right away) that it's one of his or her best efforts. This is the kind of piece that deserves real revising and editing. The revising will focus on improving word choice, organization, development, flow, and other similar elements. The editing will address conventions so that the final version includes correct spelling, punctuation, and grammar and so that the piece is typed or handwritten neatly. Only after the revising and the editing are complete will the writer have created a work that he or she can feel proud about sharing with others.

How does this process work within the classroom? As teachers, we use the Writing Workshop to model and experiment with many different types of writing for our students. Of all these drafts, we select only a few good pieces to polish through revising and editing and then to publish. There are several good reasons for this.

First, we want our students to realize that not everything they write—and certainly not everything a teacher writes—is worthy of publishing. Learning to evaluate and critique one's own work is a valuable skill. By modeling our own selection process, we help students begin to develop an internal set of criteria for discerning which of their work is not that good, which is okay, which is pretty good, and which is outstanding.

Second, if we published everything that students wrote, the process would be overwhelming for them. Putting their hearts and minds into all phases of the somewhat laborious writing process for every piece of writing would be unwieldy and impractical. On the other hand, helping students choose one outstanding piece among several, so that the task seems exciting rather than daunting, means they will likely be more willing to put forward the additional effort it takes to publish. And they will be proud to have the opportunity.

The same rationale applies to the overall classroom as well. Publishing only a few pieces per student makes it a more manageable undertaking for the whole class. You'd quickly be pulling out your hair if everything students wrote had to be revised and edited extensively and then published. Having all students working on pieces daily until they've produced perhaps three to five good pieces keeps the pace reasonable for everyone. And once students have each completed the three to five good pieces, you can winnow down the process further by conferencing with them individually to determine which one is the very best. This will be the one that deserves to go through the full process of revising and editing so that it can be published.

By contributing to class books, students gain pride in their work.

Exactly how do we define publishing? The broad definition is taking a piece of writing through all the phases of the writing process so that ultimately it is a clean and final, revised and edited product that is ready to be seen by others. Books are the most obvious format for publishing; they can be formal or informal. Some classes publish using computers with fancy graphics. Some even choose to go out to bookbinders who make the final product look very professional. At the other end of the spectrum, some teachers take an informal approach and have their students simply fold and staple pages to form booklets.

Beyond books, there are numerous ways to publish student work for others to see. Below are three of these possibilities:

1. Students can write personal letters that are actually mailed and delivered to the addressee.

2. You can display their work in classrooms or in school hallways. For instance, you might create a permanent bulletin board (see photos at right) on which students have assigned spaces to display their compositions for teachers, the principal, other students, parents, and staff members. This bulletin board should include a comment sheet for readers to write their own positive responses.

3. Students can create newsletters that can be sent home or delivered to other classes.

Students' research is proudly displayed.

The most important unifying factor in publishing is that others will get to read the students' work. This is a tremendous reward and motivator for beginning student writers.

It's worth noting that the basic revising and editing tools called on within the following lessons should already be familiar to students. Sections 1, 4, and 5 of this book have already presented the basics of revising and editing. Here, however, the focus is the inverse of what it was there—while in the earlier sections the emphasis was on the tools themselves, here the focus is on putting familiar tools and processes to use to polish a special piece of writing. The activities and lessons in this section represent the culmination of all that has gone before. As such, they can be a lot of fun. We hope you and your students enjoy your polishing and publishing endeavors!

Author's chairs give confidence to young writers as they share their writing with the class.

Editing with resources

EXPLANATION: Unlike rough-draft writing, publishing is the time for perfecting. This lesson will help students understand why this is the appropriate time for using classroom resources. It also helps you produce graphics for display to help students more easily remember what they learn here.

Skill Focus

Using appropriate references when editing—including a dictionary, books, and a simple thesaurus

Materials & Resources

☆ Dictionary, thesaurus, encyclopedia, nonfiction book, such as a content area book (suggested for this lesson: science textbook)

☆ Five sentence strips prepared ahead of time (see Step 4)

Quick Hints

As a follow-up, post the lesson's sentence strips in your classroom's Publishing Center or in the resource area next to the name of the resource that would be used. These posted strips can serve as continuing reminders to students as they need assistance.

STEPS

1. Tell students, "Boys and girls, we have many books in this classroom that will help to make our writing better. These books will be in our Publishing Center, and I want you to think about which book to use and when you'll need it. We've talked about all of these books before. They are the books published authors use."

2. On the chalkboard or a transparency, review what the books are called and what their main purposes are. Here's a sample list:

   √ **Dictionary**—helps us find correct spellings, pronunciations, background information, and usage facts about words

   √ **Thesaurus**—suggests better or more interesting words to use to replace a word we've chosen (offers both synonyms and antonyms)

   √ **Encyclopedia**—gives us in-depth information about a subject (includes many topics)

   √ **Nonfiction book**—provides factual information about a topic (usually includes related topics)

3. Place students into five small groups. Distribute to each group a sentence strip with one of the following statements:

   I need to check my spelling before I publish this piece.

   I can't seem to think of a good word to use instead of this one while I'm writing.

   I've used this word too many times and need to find another one before I publish.

   I need more facts about turtles before I finish my writing.

   I don't think this information on the salt marsh is correct and I remember we studied it last week.

4. Allow each group a few minutes to discuss which resource book or books they would check if they needed the help indicated on the sentence strip. Circulate around the room, helping to clarify students' response before they present their sentence strip and responses to the class. (Note that several groups may come up with the same answer because some references—for instance, the dictionary and the thesaurus, or the encyclopedia and a nonfiction book—represent overlapping resource categories.)

5. Finally, invite each group to stand and share its sentence strip. Each group should hold up the book or books students feel would be the best resource(s) for them to use and briefly explain why.

Two-Part Lesson: Using a Simple Checklist for Revising and Editing

Part 1: Revising

EXPLANATION: Because we hope that student writing will be as correct as possible for publishing, we need to guide students through the revision and editing steps of the writing process. The revision of the content precedes the editing phase, and that is the focus of this lesson.

Skill Focus

Using a simple checklist for revising and editing

Materials & Resources

☆ Prepared display chart or transparency of Revision Checklist (see Appendix, page 126)

☆ A transparency of a piece of your own writing that is still in rough draft stage but that you deem suitable for publishing

Quick Hints

Encourage students to keep a copy of the Revision Checklist in their writing notebooks or portfolios for quick reference. They will thus be able to carry this helpful tool with them wherever they might need it— for example, at home or in a resource class.

STEPS

1. Using a transparency, share with students a paragraph you have written previously. It should still be in first-draft stage. Below is a sample paragraph:

The Snowy Drive

The drive was short, but the snow packed highway slowed us down. Pat, Jenny and I were on our way to a snow festivul in north hills. Would we make it in time? The snowplows were working hard, but the snow was falling too quickly. The winds picked up and more snow was predicted. We had to decide. Would we keep driving and risk having a car accident? Would we turn around and head back home. Out of nowhere, a pine tree branch, heavy with snow, fell across the road right in front of our car. In that few seconds our minds were made up. We headed back home.

2. Post a prepared display chart or use a transparency to present to students a Revision Checklist (Appendix, page 126). Review the steps one by one with students. Explain that writers need to check a composition against this list as they prepare it for publishing.

3. Use your paragraph to model the process of revision. Below are sample comments you might make during a think aloud about this paragraph. Check each part of the list as you talk about it.

> *I really like my ideas, but a better sequence for this story would probably be to tell where we were driving to in the first sentence. I feel that I do have a clear beginning, middle, and end. But I see a way that I can improve my story: by adding the example about how the drive seemed like 200 miles, I'll make my writing sound more like me. I've used statements, questions, and exclamatory sentences where appropriate. Some of my sentences are long and some are short.*

4. Below is a sample revised version of the paragraph in Step 1. The revision is based on the comments in the think aloud, Step 3.

The Snowy Drive

Pat, Jenny and I were on our way to a snow festivul in north hills. The drive was only 40 miles, but it seemed like 200. short, but The snow packed highway slowed us down. Would we make it in time? The snowplows were working hard, but the snow was falling too quickly. The winds picked up and more snow was predicted. We had to decide. Would we keep driving and risk having a car accident? Would we turn around and head back home. Out of nowhere, a pine tree branch, heavy with snow, fell across the road right in front of our car. In that few seconds our minds were made up. We headed back home.

Two-Part Lesson: Using a Simple Checklist for Revising and Editing
Part 2: Editing

EXPLANATION: Helping students to refine and correct their writing in preparation for publishing involves the two steps of revision and editing. In Part 1 of this lesson, we focused on the process of revising. In this part, we review the conventions of grammar, spelling, and punctuation and help students learn how to make their final pieces as correct as possible.

Skill Focus

Using a simple checklist for revising and editing

Materials & Resources

☆ Prepared display chart or transparency of Final Editing Checklist (see Appendix, page 126)

☆ Transparency of the revised passage from Part 1 of this lesson (page 102)

Quick Hints

Have students work in small groups to explore the criteria for revision and editing. Provide an example of student writing (with that student's permission) and ask each group to discuss the piece, comparing it to the two checklists to determine if the writer met the criteria.

STEPS

1. Tell students that now that you've revised your draft (see Part 1 of this lesson), the emphasis shifts to editing. Review with the class that editing is the process writers use to make the spelling, grammar, and punctuation correct. Explain that during this step, they will need to refer to the Final Editing Checklist (see Appendix, page 126). As with the Revision Checklist, you might provide this list to students in one or more formats—for example, as a permanent display chart in the classroom and as a photocopied handout for students' writing folders.

2. Using a transparency, read through the draft from Part 1 with students. Model your editing process, saying something like the following as you go through the piece: "Now that we have made the writing better by revising, we need to use our Final Editing Checklist to be sure the writing is clean and correct. North Hills is the name of a town, so it needs to be capitalized. I see that I have two stray words left. I'd better cross them out. I did remember to capitalize the beginning of each sentence and the names of people. But I see that I need to add a question mark to a sentence that asks a question, and I need to add an exclamation mark to the sentence that shows excitement. I'll check the dictionary for the correct spelling of *festival*. I need to think about my word choice as I read my writing aloud. Yes, I think it is OK. All of my ideas were about the drive through the snow. I think I am now ready to publish." A corrected version of the story is below:

The Snowy Drive
Pat, Jenny, and I were on our way to a snow festival in North Hills. The drive was only 40 miles, but it seemed like 200. The snow packed highway slowed us down. Would we make it in time? The snowplows were working hard, but the snow was falling too quickly. The winds picked up and more snow was predicted. We had to decide. Would we keep driving and risk having a car accident? Would we turn around and head back home? Out of nowhere, a pine tree branch, heavy with snow, fell across the road right in front of our car! In that few seconds our minds were made up. We headed back home.

Using technology (word processing)

EXPLANATION: Many state standards require that students become competent in using technology. In second and third grade, students are asked to demonstrate knowledge and skill in basic computer word processing.

Skill Focus

Using technology, including word processing software

Materials & Resources

☆ Computers; disc for each student

☆ Student interviews conducted previously (see Step 1 and Quick Hints)

Quick Hints

As preparation for this lesson on computer use, as well as to give students experience with the process of interviewing, pair students and have each student in a pair interview the other. Be sure students write down their answers as clear notes that they will be able to use later for their paragraphs. Here are suggested questions you might provide for students to use for their interviews:

Who are the members of your family?

If you could have any animal for a pet, what would you ask for and why?

Why do you like to come to school?

What after-school activity is one of your favorites?

STEPS

Note: *This lesson is best taught in small groups; you might have other students participate in the Writing Workshop while you teach each individual group at the computer. Alternately, you might teach this lesson to the whole class in a school computer lab.*

1. Tell students that in this lesson they will be using the computer to write short paragraphs based on the interviews they conducted previously (see Quick Hints). Note that student paragraphs could be based on almost any short assignment; we recommend interviews because they are engaging and involve students in conversation to precede the writing.

2. Use the following steps (appropriate for most major Windows-based programs) to guide the students in their word processing:

   ☆ Start the word processing program.

   ☆ Open/start a new document and choose a font, font size, and color.

   ☆ Ask students to type the titles of their papers, using correct finger placement. To center the titles on the page, show students how to highlight the title and then left-click on the "center" icon in the formatting bar at the top of the screen. Then have them type their first sentence, after first using the space bar to indent five spaces. Remind students how to use the shift key for capitalizing, the delete key, and the arrow keys to navigate through their writing.

   ☆ Calling on their writing process skills as well as their experience with crafting paragraphs, ask students to type in brief compositions based on their interview notes.

   ☆ Show students how to double-space their paragraphs by using Select All (Ctrl+A), then clicking the Ctrl button and the number 2.

   ☆ When they are finished, ask students to click File, then "save as" to name their file and save it, either to the hard drive or to a disc.

   ☆ At the end of the session, have students click File and select Print, click OK, and then click Yes to print their paragraphs.

3. Have students revise and edit their work on paper, perhaps during an individual conference.

4. When students have finished editing, ask them to open their files again, make revisions and editing changes within the word-processing program, and print out their final documents.

Sharing writing orally with others

EXPLANATION: Sharing gives students an opportunity to try out their writing on an audience. The feedback they receive can motivate them to revise. The audience also receives ideas and a brief time to reflect on writing. And the teacher can use this time to observe and evaluate.

Skill Focus

Sharing writing with others

Materials & Resources

☆ A piece of your own writing that you know could benefit from revising

Quick Hints

Delight your students with a special day each grading period in which you invite an adult (school staff, district staff, parent, etc.) to share a piece of writing. (Teachers frequently invite guests to come in to read aloud from time to time, so why not have the guest come in to share his or her own writing?)

Plan small-group sharing sessions for those who are shy and those who need practice in how to make constructive comments about writing.

STEPS

1. Explain the purposes of sharing one's writing orally. Tell the class that both the author and the audience benefit: Writers receive valuable feedback that can help guide their revising, and the listeners have a chance to really think about what makes a piece of writing good.

2. Model how to share one's writing. Introduce your sharing by announcing a specific request—something you would especially like the listeners to pay attention to. For example, you might say to the audience, "I would like you to listen to the beginning of my piece and tell me what you think about it."

3. Read aloud a short excerpt from the piece of writing. Encourage responses from your student audience, making sure they focus their comments on the angle you requested.

4. Discuss how you feel about their feedback and what you plan to do in response to those comments. For example, you might say, "Your idea about beginning my piece by describing the setting sounds like something I would like to try. I will rewrite the first two or three sentences to fit this type of lead."

5. Finally, have student volunteers select and share orally their own writing. Be sure to have students keep the writing they read aloud to short, focused excerpts; to ask the audience ahead of time to focus on specific aspects about the writing; and to end their reading by describing a plan of action.

Four-Part Lesson: Publishing a Nonfiction Book

Part 1: Selecting a topic and getting started

> **EXPLANATION:** In the first of this multi-part lesson, each student chooses a specific topic (from related topics within one designated subject) that he or she will write and publish a book about and begins the research.

Skill Focus

Publishing a nonfiction book

Materials & Resources

☆ Nonfiction texts (suggested titles: *Amazing Animals* by Kate Boehm Nyquist; *The Big Book of Animals* by Sheila Hanly; *The National Geographic Animal Encyclopedia, They Walk the Earth* by Simone Seymour; *Ranger Rick* Magazine; *Journey Into the Artic* by Bryan and Cherry Alexander; *Small Worlds: On the Tundra* by Jen Green)

☆ Websites to visit:
www.natzoo.si.edu;
www.montereybayaquarium.org;
www.exploratorium.org

Quick Hints

Work with your school's media specialist to hold book talks on nonfiction books within the nonfiction section of the media center. Once the student-created books are complete, they can be displayed next to the nonfiction books in the media center. This helps students to feel like "real" authors!

Preliminary Considerations:

For several weeks before you begin this multi-part publishing lesson, make a point of displaying many nonfiction texts prominently in the classroom. During this period, read aloud several of these books. Explicitly call attention to how these books, magazines, and other resources might serve as examples of nonfiction text structure and topics for writing.

We recommend that a science unit guide the selection of topics for this lesson because the study of science is filled with interesting facts and engages the interest of almost all students. Many second- and third-grade classrooms include the study of animals in their science curriculum; for this reason, we have chosen the subject of vertebrate animals as the model content for this lesson.

STEPS

1. Introduce this lesson by telling the class that several days of Writing Workshop will be devoted to publishing individual books. Explain to students that the books will be based on the nonfiction texts they have been listening to, looking at, and reading independently in the classroom for the past several weeks.

2. Tell students that, based on these nonfiction texts, you want them to create a list of possible topics for their own books. Allow time for browsing and discussion among partners or the whole class before continuing. With the class, on a transparency or chart paper, jot down a list of possible topics resulting from the discussions. For our model subject of vertebrate animals, a sample list follows:

   Amazing Animal Facts
   All About Birds (or Reptiles, Insects, etc.)
   Animals That Live in the Desert
   Animals That Live in the Ocean
   Animals That Adapt to their Environment
   How Animals Survive
   Different Kinds of Animals That Have Backbones

3. Tell each student that he or she needs to select a topic to research. When all students have chosen their topics, help them to form groups based on the topics.

4. Invite these groups of students to begin going through the available texts and resources to find facts about their topics. As students find facts about their topic, have them write down key words describing these facts on a piece of paper.

Four-Part Lesson: Publishing a Nonfiction Book

Parts 2 and 3: **Researching and sharing**

> **EXPLANATION:** In the second and third parts of this multi-part lesson, students use various nonfiction texts to research and categorize facts for their own books.

Skill Focus

Publishing a nonfiction book

Materials & Resources

☆ Nonfiction resources from Part 1 of this lesson

☆ File folders

☆ Sticky notes in three different colors

Quick Hints

Always model the type of interaction you hope to achieve through sharing. Students may share with a peer, small group, or with the whole class. Designate a special chair or area for students to use during sharing time. Model how you might share new facts learned and allow the class to ask clarifying questions.

Remind students that this stage of writing is called a draft. Use the rule that Nancie Atwell has in her classroom: No Erasing! Just change by crossing out and keep going. Not only will this result in a complete record of ideas, but time spent off task will be reduced.

STEPS (Part 2)

1. Continue to allow students to research facts from the various nonfiction texts you have gathered and made available—trade books, science books, science encyclopedias, magazines, and so on, as well as from the Internet.

2. Provide a "share chair" for students to share interesting facts they learn through the research. (See Quick Hints.)

STEPS (Part 3)

1. Provide a set of sticky notes in three colors to each student. Explain that students need to organize all the facts they have collected before they can write their books. Like facts (facts that fit into the same category) are to be written on the same color of sticky note, one fact for each sticky note. Facts that fit into a second category should be included on sticky notes of a different color. And facts that are still different should be written on the sticky notes of the third color.

2. After introducing the task, model for students how to do the categorizing. Using the topic in the example below, demonstrate how you categorize facts concerning that topic. First write the name of your topic and list the facts you have found under that heading. Then, using a set of differently-colored sticky notes, categorize each fact and rewrite it on an appropriately colored sticky note. Place that sticky note next to the note on your original list.

Topic: Different Kinds of Animals with Backbones
Facts: These animals are called vertebrates. (yellow note)
   The bones in the backbone are called vertebra. (yellow note)
   Dogs and cats are vertebrates with hair. (blue note)
   Frogs are amphibians and amphibians are vertebrates. (green note)
   Part of a frog's life is spent in water and part on land. (green note)
   Mammals live everywhere on earth. (blue note)

Think aloud throughout this process, naming the three categories your facts fit into:

   Yellow: definition and traits of vertebrates; *Blue*: characteristics of mammals; *Green*: characteristics of amphibians

3. Now move the sticky notes and reposition them so that all same-colored notes are grouped together.

4. Finally, have students write their own facts on colored sticky notes, categorizing them as you have demonstrated. Circulate around the room, checking to make sure that students are organizing their facts appropriately.

Four-Part Lesson: Publishing a Nonfiction Book

Part 4: Typing and assembling

EXPLANATION: In the final part of this multi-part lesson, students experience the fruition of the previous days' work as they type their notes and then assemble and bind them into books.

Skill Focus

Publishing a nonfiction book

Materials & Resources

☆ File folders containing categorized sticky notes from Part 3 of this lesson

☆ Notebook paper

☆ Colorful construction or poster paper

☆ Staples, glue, string, or other bookbinding material

Quick Hints

String a fishing line, heavy string, or thin rope across a bulletin board, wall, or writing corner. Drape student books over the line or rope so that the covers face outward and the books are in easy reach for independent reading time.

STEPS

1. Tell students that in the final part of this lesson, they will be creating their own nonfiction books from their categorized facts. Begin by having students gather the sticky notes from their file folders. Instruct them to neatly write or type one fact on each page. They may position the fact at the top or bottom of the page—in either case, leaving most of the page blank (for illustrations or photos). Explain to students that these facts are now the core of their nonfiction books, providing the information about their topic that they want to share with an audience.

2. Tell students that their nonfiction books need illustrations in order to be truly helpful to readers. Model how you might illustrate one of the pages. For example, you might use computer-generated clipart or photographs from magazines, or you might create original drawings.

3. Have students work in pairs or small groups to brainstorm other possible pages for their books. Circulate among the groups, encouraging students to list possibilities such as: cover; dedication; table of contents; introduction of several sentences; summary composed of several sentences; author biography page.

4. Depending upon time and resources available, have pairs or groups select a few of these possible pages to create. For example, students might look through dedication pages in published books in order to get ideas for their own dedication. And to make book covers, they might use decorated construction paper or cardboard covered with gift wrapping paper.

5. When the books are complete, have students staple or otherwise bind the pages (for instance, they might hole-punch the left-hand margin and tie it with yarn). Now the books are ready to be proudly displayed in the classroom—for instance, shelved with other nonfiction books in the classroom library or tacked up on a bulletin board. Or, see Quick Hints for a way to display the books with a bit of flair!

Publishing in various formats

EXPLANATION: Publishing doesn't have to be done in book format. In this lesson, the focus is on an interactive bulletin board display that allows readers to comment on a piece of writing and communicate their (positive) reactions directly to the writer.

Skill Focus

Publishing in various formats

Materials & Resources

☆ Student composition that is ready to publish (with student's prior permission to use this work)

☆ One plastic sheet protector (for future writing displays, you'll need one for each student)

☆ Transparency made from Writing Comment Sheet (see Step 4 below)

☆ Bulletin board space in the classroom or in the hallway

Quick Hints

During sharing time, encourage students to go to the display board, select one piece of writing, and bring it back to their table to read. Using the Comment Sheet, they should then write a positive comment. Invite other staff and faculty to come by and read a few pieces of writing as often as they can and write a brief comment.

STEPS

1. Create a bulletin board display that has sufficient space for all students in your class to exhibit a piece of work. (See photos on page 99 for two examples.) Tell students something like this: "You'll each be assigned your own personal space on our writing display board where you'll keep one of your best writing pieces. We'll invite many people to read what we've written and to share—in a special spot right on the bulletin board—their positive comments about the writing. I'll also be giving you time to read your friends' writing and to share your comments. We'll have fun reading what other students think of our writing."

2. Tell students you will demonstrate for them the kinds of comments they might make about their friends' writing. Explain that one of the students in the class has agreed ahead of time to have his/her composition read aloud.

3. Read aloud the previously agreed-upon student composition. Afterward, you might say something like, "Jason did a really great job of telling us about his trip to the Grand Canyon, didn't he? I'm going to write a note to him to tell him what I liked best about this piece. I think what I liked best was his description of the canyon. He used words that let me get a picture in my mind of exactly what he saw. I'll tell him that." You may want to remind students about the skill of how to provide positive feedback, which they studied in the Sharing Writing Orally lesson (page 105).

4. Using a transparency of the Writing Comment Sheet at right, fill in an appropriate commentary. (Note that in the example below, the template for the Comment Sheet is shown in boldface. The words filled in on the lines are specific to this example.)

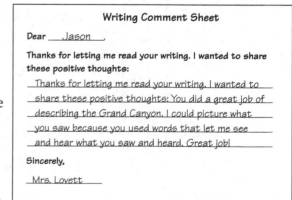

Writing Comment Sheet

Dear ___Jason___,

Thanks for letting me read your writing. I wanted to share these positive thoughts:

Thanks for letting me read your writing. I wanted to
share these positive thoughts: You did a great job of
describing the Grand Canyon. I could picture what
you saw because you used words that let me see
and hear what you saw and heard. Great job!

Sincerely,

Mrs. Lovett

5. Explain that the Comment Sheets are stored right with the student's piece of writing. You might say, "Now, I'll slip my Comments Sheet behind Jason's story so that he can read these comments any time he wants to check his folder. Won't it be fun to know that other people will be reading your writing and writing to you?" Tuck the Comment Sheet behind the student composition, and put both in the sheet protector. Finally, staple the sheet protector packet to the bulletin board with the other students' folders.

Spelling Strategies

1.

Find it in the room.

2.

Think what it sounds like.

3.

Think of parts I know.

Th + ing

4.

Think of letter sounds and stretch it out.

5.

Think whether I've seen it before.

Word	Strategy	Word	Strategy	Word	Strategy
1.		5.		9.	
2.		6.		10.	
3.		7.		11.	
4.		8.		12.	

Directions for Making a Kaleidoscope

MATERIALS:

- ☆ Clear 35 mm film container with lid (usually free at one-hour film stores)
- ☆ Mirrored paper board
- ☆ Stiff clear plastic disk or plastic wrap
- ☆ Small, colorful items such as: crayon shavings, cake sprinkles, beads, etc.
- ☆ Tape

INSTRUCTIONS:

1. Using a clear film container, drill a hole about a 1/4-inch in diameter in the bottom for the eye hole.

2. Cut a piece of mirror board (from local craft store) 1 3/4-inches by 3 inches.

3. Fold to make a triangle with the mirror side to the inside.

4. Tape it to hold the triangle shape and insert it inside the film container.

5. Put 6 to 7 very small items in the indentation of the inside of the lid.

6. Cover with a piece of stiff plastic the size of a quarter or with plastic wrap.

7. Place the cylinder onto the lid and snap into place.

8. Point it up into the light and turn. (You may need to adjust the number of items.)

Alphabet Chart

Topic:	A	B	C	D
E	F	G	H	I
J	K	L	M	N
O	P	Q	R	S
T	U	V	W	X Y Z

Name _____

Questions for Investigating Worksheet

My Questions About _____	Other Students' Questions	My Final Questions

Writing Graphic Organizer

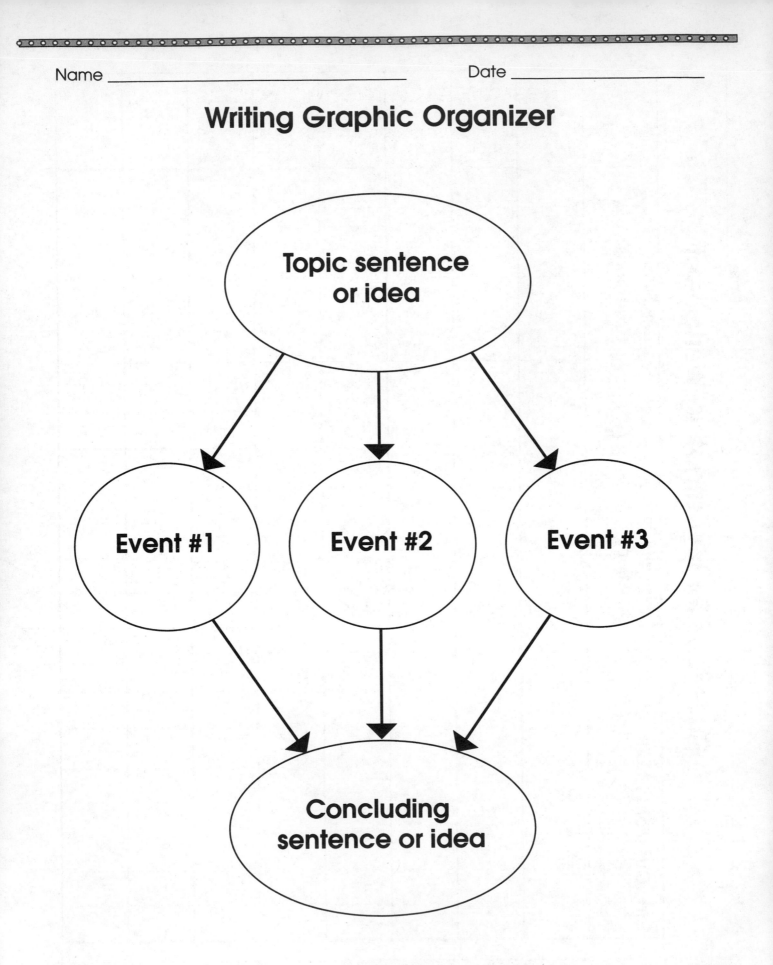

Just-Right Writing Mini-Lessons: Grades 2–3 SCHOLASTIC TEACHING RESOURCES

Resource Gathering Forms

Use these forms to gather information from resource material.

Book:

Author:

Title:

City:

Publisher:

Date:

Magazine:

Article title:

Magazine:

Month:

Year:

Page numbers:

World Wide Web site:

Author's Name:

Full title in quotation marks:

Date of publication:

Full http address: < >

Date of visit: ( )

Transparency Master for Punctuation Activity*

So everyone was happy when Ms. Frizzle announced Today we start something new We are going to study about our earth said Ms. Frizzle She put us to work writing reports about earth science And for homework she said each person must find a rock and bring it to school But the next day almost everyone had some excuse

*excerpt (with missing punctuation) from *The Magic School Bus Inside the Earth* by Joanna Cole

Just-Right Writing Mini-Lessons: Grades 2–3 SCHOLASTIC TEACHING RESOURCES

Name _____   Date _____

Sequencing Chart

Clue words for time order	Events

Imagery Chart

Imagery Language	Classification

Use these imagery language classifications:

- ☆ Similes
- ☆ Metaphors
- ☆ Sensory details
- ☆ Action verbs

- ☆ Adjectives
- ☆ Adverbs
- ☆ Concrete examples

Letter Puzzle #1

1601 Northside Drive

Penelope, SC 61111

Jennifer

July 14, 2005

I hope you'll write back soon! Tell your family hello for me!

Summer has been so much fun! I wanted to tell you about one adventure this past weekend. We went to a state park in South Carolina called Huntington Beach. It has Palmetto trees, white sandy beaches, and lots of shells. We got up early each morning and collected sand dollars, conches, and many other beautiful shells. On Saturday, I was stung by a jellyfish, but I was soon back in the water jumping the waves! Both nights we cooked out on the beach. I hated for the weekend to end!

Please let me know what you're doing this summer. Have you read any books? I know you enjoy doing that, and I do, too. Have you taken any trips? Let me know about your dog and what tricks you've taught him now.

Continued on next page

Dear Jerri | Your friend | , | ,

Jerri

Letter Puzzle #2

August 2, 2005

How are you? I am fine. I have had a good summer. We went to the beach and to the mountains. I'm looking forward to starting third grade later this month.

Oldtown, PA 16662

I hope you'll write back to me soon.

Dear Jennifer

161 Beltline Avenue

Your friend | , | ,

Persuasive Letter Plan Template

Focus on the audience of the writing.
Who is the letter written to?

State your opinion, idea, or point of view.

Write support for your opinion. (Include at least 3 reasons.)

1. _____

2. _____

3. _____

Restate your opinion.

5 W's with Group Cut-outs

I. Leads, in sentence form, for the teacher:

Thomas Headley, a student at City High School, was attacked by a flock of birds at Pennington Park on Saturday, May 20, because he ran out of the bread he was feeding them.

On Saturday, June 6th, a stray dog became a hero by pulling a drowning child from the water at Boyd's Pond.

Tickles, a clown with the Dalton Circus, had an unexpected ride during Tuesday night's parade in Oven's Coliseum, since he became entangled in an elephant's rope.

During its meeting on September 16 at the Nock Middle School, the school board defeated a proposal to remove vending machines from five schools, citing that the machines brought needed funding.

The Brownsville Bobcats won the season opener on Monday night at Memorial Stadium, pouncing on the Edgetown Tornadoes, 21–10.

II. For the students to cut apart:

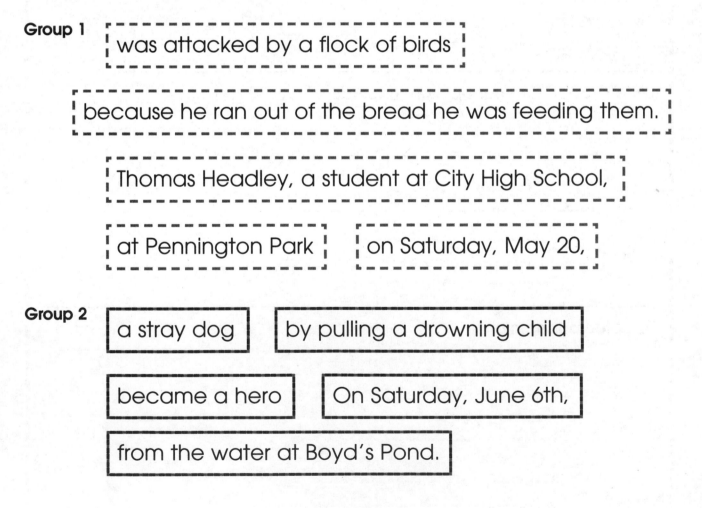

Group 1

was attacked by a flock of birds

because he ran out of the bread he was feeding them.

Thomas Headley, a student at City High School,

at Pennington Park

on Saturday, May 20,

Group 2

a stray dog

by pulling a drowning child

became a hero

On Saturday, June 6th,

from the water at Boyd's Pond.

Just-Right Writing Mini-Lessons: Grades 2–3 SCHOLASTIC TEACHING RESOURCES

Group 3

during Tuesday night's parade

had an unexpected ride

in Oven's Coliseum,

Tickles, a clown with the Dalton Circus,

since he became entangled in an elephant's rope.

Group 4

the school board

at the Nock Middle School,

citing that the machines brought needed funding.

defeated a proposal to remove vending machines from five schools,

During its meeting on September 16

Group 5

on Monday night

pouncing on the Edgetown Tornadoes, 21–10.

won the season opener

at Memorial Stadium,

The Brownsville Bobcats

BOOK-O
Book Report Matrix

Write a summary.	Write a new beginning or ending.	Write entries in a character journal.
Develop a character interview.	Give a book talk.	Write a bio-poem of a character.
Retell the story from a character's point of view.	Write a letter to the author telling why you liked the book.	Design an advertisement for the book (sell the book to the class).

Book Report Assessment

Student name _____ Date _____

Title of book _____

Author _____

Oral presentation	30 points	Comments:
☆ Poise	5 points	
☆ Eye contact	5 points	
☆ Clarity of voice/ projection	5 points	
☆ Content	15 points	**Score** _____
Written presentation	**30 points**	**Comments:**
☆ Organized	5 points	
☆ Correct grammar and mechanics	5 points	
☆ Content	20 points	**Score** _____
Time frame 3–5 minutes	**5 points**	**Score** _____
Total score	**65 points**	**Score** _____

Revision Checklist

I read my writing out loud.

    To myself _____   To a friend _____   To a group _____

I asked if my writing made sense. _____

My writing was organized with a beginning, middle, and end. _____

My ideas were developed and appropriately sequenced. _____

I stayed focused on the topic. _____

I used a variety of sentence types and lengths. _____

My writing sounded like me. (voice) _____

- -

Final Editing Checklist

I used capitals in the right places. _____

I ended each sentence with a **.**, **!**, or **?**. _____

I checked my grammar. _____

I checked my spelling. _____

I used interesting words. _____

Bibliography

Alexander, Bryan and Cherry Alexander. *Journey into the Artic*. Oxford: 2003.

Arnold, Tedd. *Parts*. NY: Puffin Books, Penguin Putnam Books, 1997.

Atwell, Nancie. Presentation at NCTE, San Diego, Nov. 1995.

Bollard, John. *Scholastic Children's Thesaurus*. NY: Scholastic, 2002.

Bradby, Marie. *More Than Anything Else*. NY: Orchard Books, 1995.

Brenner, Barbara. *If You Lived in Williamsburg in Colonial Days*. NY: Scholastic, 2000.

Calkins, Lucy and Shelley Harwayne. *Living Between the Lines*. Portsmouth, NH: Heinemann Educational Books, Inc., 1991.

Choron, Sandra and Harry Choron. *The All-New Book of Lists for Kids*. Boston: Houghton Mifflin, 2002.

Cleary, Beverly. *Dear Mr. Henshaw*. NY: Morrow, 1983.

Cole, Joanna. *The Magic School Bus Inside the Earth*. NY: Scholastic, 1987.

Cole, Joanna. *The Magic School Bus Inside the Human Body*. NY: Scholastic, 1990.

Cushman, Karen. *Catherine, Called Birdy*. NY: Harper, 1994.

Dyson, A. H. and S.W. Freedman. "Writing." In J. Flood, D. Lapp, J. R. Squire, and J. M. Jensen (Eds.), *Handbook of research on teaching the English language arts* (2nd ed.; pp. 967-992). Mahwah, NJ: Erlbaum, 2003.

Farnan, N. and K. Dahl. "Children's writing: Research and practice." In J. Flood, D. Lapp, J. R. Squire, and J. M. Jensen (Eds.), *Handbook of research on teaching the English language arts* (2nd ed.; pp. 993-1007). Mahwah, NJ: Erlbaum, 2003.

Fletcher, Ralph. *What a Writer Needs*. Portsmouth, NH: Heinemann, 1993.

Fletcher, Ralph and JoAnn Portalupi. *Writing Workshop: the Essential Guide*. Portsmouth, NH: Heinemann, 2001.

Fountas, Irene and Gay Su Pinnell. *Guiding Readers and Writers: Grades 3–6*. Portsmouth, NH: Heinemann, 2001.

Frost, Robert and Susan Jeffers. *Stopping by Woods on a Snowy Evening*. NY: Dutton Children's Books.

Gibbons, Gail. *The Moon Book*. NY: Holiday House, 1997.

Goble, Paul. *Dream Wolf*. NY: Simon and Schuster, 1997.

Goodall, Jane. *Dr. White*. NY: North-South Books, 1999.

Green, Jen. *Small Worlds: On the Tundra*. NY: Crabtree, 2002.

Hanly, Sheila. *The Big Book of Animals*. NY: DK Publications, 1997

Harvey, Stephanie. *Non-Fiction Matters*. York, ME: Stenhouse, 1998.

Hewitt, Sally. *It's Science! Full of Energy*. Danbury, CT: Children's Press, Grolier Publications, 1998.

Hillocks, G., Jr. "Synthesis of Research of Teaching Writing." *Educational Leadership*, 1987.

Hillocks, G., Jr. "Research on written composition: New directions for teaching." Urbana, IL: National Conference on Research in English/ERIC Clearinghouse on Reading and Communication Skills, 1986.

Hillocks, G., Jr. and M.W. Smith. "Grammar and literacy learning." In J. Flood, D. Lapp, J. R. Squire, and J. M. Jensen (Eds.), *Handbook of research on teaching the English language arts* (2nd ed.; pp. 721-737). Mahwah, NJ: Erlbaum, 2003.

Hodges, R. E. "The conventions of writing." In J. Flood, D. Lapp, J. R. Squire, and J. M. Jensen (Eds.), *Handbook of research on teaching the English language arts* (2nd ed.; pp. 1052-1063). Mahwah, NJ: Erlbaum, 2003.

Houston, Gloria. *My Great-Aunt Arizona*. NY: HarperCollins Publishers, 1992.

Kellogg, Steven. *The Mysterious Tadpole*. NY: Dial Books for Young Readers, Penguin Putnam, 2002.

Manning, Mick and Brita Granstorm. *Splish, Splash, Splosh*. NY: Franklin Watts, 1997.

McNaughton, Colin. *Suddenly*. NY: Voyager Books, Harcourt Brace, 1998.

McCarthy, Tara. *Persuasive Writing*. Scholastic Professional Books, 1998.

Morgan, Sally. *Animals as Friends*. NY: Franklin Watts, 2000.

Moss, Marissa. *Emma's Journal: The Story of a Colonial Girl*. NY: Harcourt Brace, 1999.

Moss, Marissa. *Rachel's Journal: The Story of a Pioneer Girl*. NY: Harcourt Brace, 2001.

Munsch, Robert. *Stephanie's Ponytail*. NY: Firefly Books, 2002.

The National Geographic Animal Encyclopedia. Washington, DC: National Geographic Society, 2002.

Numeroff, Laura. *If You Give a Mouse a Cookie*. NY: HarperCollins, 1985.

Nyquist, Kate Blehm. *Amazing Animals*. Washington, DC: National Geographic Society, Reading Expeditions, 2002.

O'Neill, Amanda. *I Wonder Why Snakes Shed Their Skin and other questions about reptiles*. NY: Kingfisher, 1998.

Osborne, Mary Pope. *Stage Fright on a Summer Night*. NY: Scholastic, 2002.

Park, Barbara. *Junie B. Jones and Some Sneaky Peeky Spying*. NY: Scholastic, 1994.

Polacco, Patricia. *My Rotten Redheaded Older Brother*. NY: Aladdin Books, 1998.

Ranger Rick Magazine. NY: Scholastic.

Rylant, Cynthia. *Scarecrow*. NY: Harcourt Brace, 1998.

Sebranek, Patrick, et al. *Writers INC*. Write Source, 1996.

Seymour, Simon. *They Walk the Earth: The Extraordinary Travels of Animals on Land*. Browndeer Press, 2000.

Sigmon, Cheryl. *Modifying the Four Blocks for the Upper Grades*. Greensboro, NC: Carson-Dellosa, 2001.

Steptoe, John. *Stevie*. NY: HarperTrophy, 1986.

Stolz, Mary. *Storm in the Night*. NY: HarperTrophy, 1988.

Thimmesh, Catherine. *Girls Think of Everything: Stories of Ingenious Inventions by Women*. Boston: Houghton Mifflin, 2000.

Viorst, Judith. *Alexander and the Terrible, Horrible, No Good, Very Bad Day*. NY: Aladdin Books, 1972.

Wexo, John Bennett. "Snakes." *Zoobooks* (Jan, 1997): pp. 1–17.

Wood Ray, Katie. *Wondrous Words*. Urbana, IL: NCTE, 1999.

_____*Write Right, An English Handbook*, Phi Delta Kappa, Bloomington, IN.

Wood, Audrey and Don Wood. *Moonflute*. NY: Harcourt Brace, 1986.

Yolen, Jane. *Owl Moon*. NY: Philomel, 1987.

Websites used for information:

www.natzoo.si.edu

www.pelotes.jea.com/vensnake.htm

www.smithsonianeducation.org/students

www.montereybayaquarium.org

www.exploratorium.org

www.usps.com

http://familycrafts.about.com

Writing Graphic Organizer

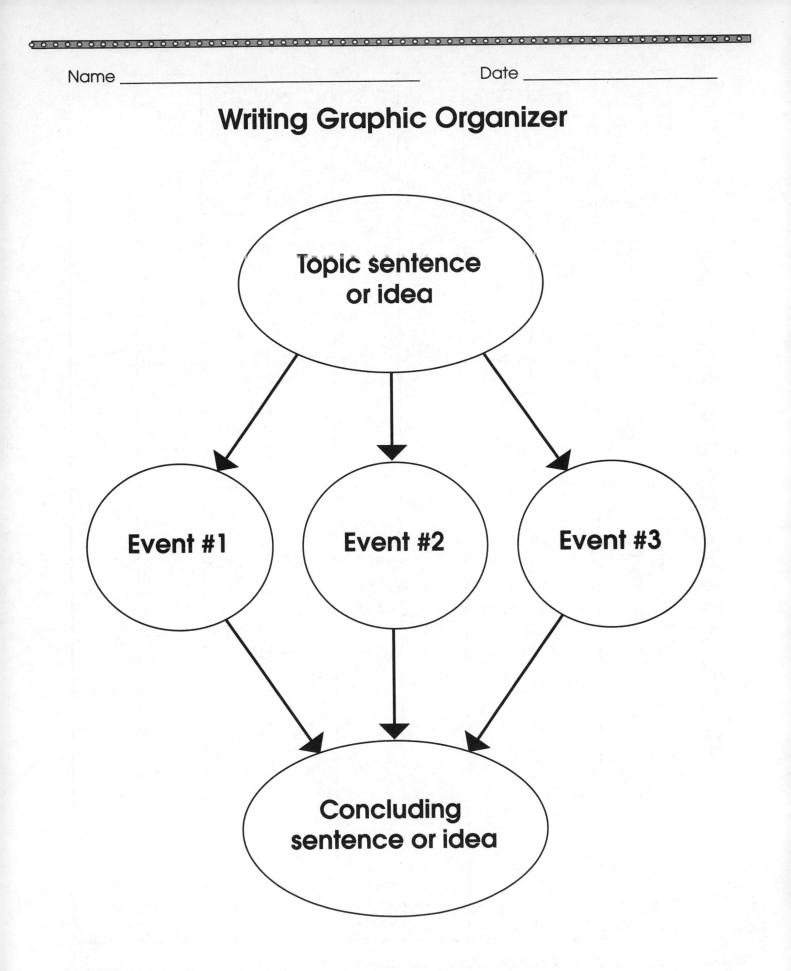

Name _____

Date _____

Questions for Investigating Worksheet

My Questions About _____	Other Students' Questions	My Final Questions